BE BILINGUAL

PRACTICAL IDEAS FOR MULTILINGUAL FAMILIES

Annika Bourgogne

Published by:
Annika Bourgogne
Copyright (c) 2013 by Annika Bourgogne

ISBN 978-952-68037-0-8

To stay in touch with us, visit

http:\\www.be-bilingual.net

Table of Contents

Acknowledgments

There are many people I want to thank for their help in making this book become reality. The first one, without a doubt, is my husband Gilles, the best partner I could ever imagine to have on our family's bilingual journey. I am so grateful for his understanding and encouragement even when I've spent hours just reading and writing in the evenings. I do realize, that I have months of cooking and laundry ahead of me to make up for all his efforts this past year.

I am not a native speaker of English, and, despite teaching it as a foreign language on a daily basis, the first draft of this book contained many errors. I want to acknowledge and thank James Perkins of Koala Consulting and Training for his valuable help with making my text more readable to others. Any mistakes that might be left are entirely my responsibility.

A big thanks also to all the families that shared their best ideas with me, as well as to those who pre-read the book, and gave helpful comments. I am also in awe of all the people who have for years written blogs and had Facebook pages and websites dedicated to promoting multilingualism. These people truly inspire me.

Finally, I am grateful for my two children, Emma and Sara, without whom this book would not have existed.

Preface

When I was a child, I would tell anyone willing to listen that I spoke Finnish, Swedish and Svenska. Had that really been the case I would have known that two of these languages were actually the same. Instead, I was in fact like most Finns: a monolingual child going to a Finnish school, aware of the existence of the two languages in the community around me, but able to speak only one of them. Yet I could have, maybe even should have, spoken both of them.

I was born in the mid-seventies to a family that had all the prerequisites for the perfect environment in which to grow up bilingual. My mother belonged to the six percent minority of Finns who spoke Swedish as their native language. Since birth, she had spoken Swedish with her mother and Finnish with her father, and was a perfect example of a bilingual who is very competent in both her languages. When at school, she was part of the Swedish group, both linguistically and culturally. The Swedish-speaking Finns have a distinct cultural identity, which is sometimes envied by the Finnish-speaking majority. My mom fit this group perfectly, but she had also learned the social codes and habits of the Finnish-speaking population from playing with her neighbors, and associated with them just as easily, with not so much as a trace of an accent to give away her other language heritage. That's how she met my dad.

My father was the second son of a wealthy Finnish-speaking family, among whom the Finnish culture and language were highly valued. I have often wondered what it was like for my mother, with the background that she had, to enter the family. The Swedish-speaking families were often wealthy, culturally active families who had a large representation among the Finnish nobility. They were the kind of families my paternal grandparents might well have perceived as an economic, cultural, or linguistic threat. No such threat was presented by my mother's family, which consisted of mainly farm workers, but still she probably stood no chance of passing on her linguistic heritage to her daughter. As a result, I became the first person in her Swedish-speaking family line to speak only Finnish at home.

The official reason for my parents raising me monolingually was far more politically correct than the family politics that I suspect to be true. In the seventies there was a lot of talk about the possible dangers of bilingualism, and how raising a child in two languages might result in serious learning disabilities - the worst-case scenario was that the child would not learn either language properly. Parents were warned about children becoming confused, their small brains not being able to handle the introduction of two languages simultaneously. Indeed, some even went so far as to claim that learning two languages might result in a split personality. All of these myths have since been debunked, and being bilingual herself, my mom really should have known better.

My maternal grandmother tried her best to speak Swedish to me, and my relatives remember that I had at least a passive knowledge of the language in my early years. At some point, she too must have given up, for the only language I have any childhood memory of her speaking to me is Finnish. Neither do I recall understanding anything my mom and grandma said to each other in Swedish. The good news is that I did hear it on a nearly daily basis during visits and phone calls. The language was always present and that made it so much easier when Swedish lessons (dreaded by many, compulsory for all) began at school. Suddenly, all those words started making sense; it was obvious that I had picked up a lot during the years without realizing it.

I put effort into learning more Swedish and it became a question of pride for me to learn the language of my maternal family. By the time I was in senior high school I was fluent in Swedish and could carry on a conversation in most subjects - in class. Outside school, I seemed to have very little use for my language skills. Whenever I found myself in a group of Swedish-speaking Finns and tried to take part in the conversation, the language was immediately changed to Finnish. It wasn't about me or my language skills, I believe, but rather a common phenomenon that many Finns who have attempted the same have encountered. Whether it was done to be polite or to judge my language skills, the message was loud and clear: I was *not* a member of their group and speaking Swedish with them was not right. Neither would my family use Swedish with me, as they claimed it was too weird. Only my grandmother did, and I have fond memories of the conversations we had in Swedish when I was staying with her for a few months to study for my matriculation exam. As a result of this, the Swedish-speaking Finns today are puzzled when they meet me, and don't know where to place me. They still know I'm not one of them and speak Finnish to me. Invariably, though, they ask me where I learned my Swedish.

Introduction

With my background, I was curious about bilingualism and bilinguals from the beginning – because I wasn't one! Even later, when I learned several languages to varying degrees of fluency, I never labeled myself as bilingual. To me at that time, and I have since then broadened my definition significantly, only children having learned two languages from birth and able to speak both with equal ease were bilingual.

When I met and eventually married Gilles, a Frenchman who was completing his degree in papermaking in Finland, the possibility of bicultural children started to seem destined. The decision to raise them to be bilingual as well was an easy one, at least for me – I didn't want my children to have the same feeling of missing out on their cultural and linguistic heritage that I'd always had. Gilles agreed that once we had children he would speak to them in French, so that they would be able to communicate with his family back in France. This was all the planning that we felt was necessary to raise children who, in our minds, would be "perfect bilinguals", which we at that time believed to mean two monolinguals in one person.

What made me realize that there was more to the matter than just deciding to speak our own native languages to our future children, was a coincidental meeting with another French-Finnish family. Walking in downtown Helsinki one Saturday, we came across a family that resided in France and was on holiday in Finland. We started talking, and as I admired their two beautiful children, I asked the mother if she spoke Finnish with them. Encouraged by her affirmative answer, I addressed the children in Finnish.

Reluctantly, they answered, and it was very clear that they were not at ease speaking the language; they sounded like French children that had learned a few words of Finnish. At the first opportunity, they switched back to French. The parents beamed, but I was confused, as it was not what I had expected based on my experience with Swedish-speaking Finns. This encounter stayed with me and was one of the reasons that I chose bilingualism as the subject of my master's thesis at university the following year. I wanted to find out what factors contributed to the level of bilingualism I hoped our children would have. By this time, I knew that this level could also be reached by children speaking Finnish and French and had arranged to interview such families for my studies.

My thesis

The first summer Gilles and I were married, he stayed behind in Finland to work on his thesis while I spent two months in France with my in-laws, traveling back and forth to meet the families that participated in my study. The objective of my research was to study, in a very concrete manner, what needed to be done in order to successfully raise bilingual children. Part of the study was based on general literature on the subject, and another part consisted of case studies, meeting families that spoke both French and Finnish at home, and who were raising their children to speak (at least) both of these languages. All the families had children that were between 10 and 12 years old, and their written and oral skills in both languages were compared to the answers the parents had given in interviews about their family's situation, and the different ways they had facilitated and encouraged their children's bilingualism. Similar interviews with families in comparable situations were also conducted in Finland at a later date.

The results of the study were very interesting, not only academically, but on a personal level, too. They confirmed what is common knowledge in the field today, but wasn't perhaps quite as emphasized in the literature of the time: unlike the **community language** (in other words the **majority language** or the language that is present in the daily living environment), the **non-community language** (also called the **minority language**), needs a lot of reinforcement for children to speak it fluently. Among the children that participated in the study, the level of their non-community language seemed to be directly proportional to the efforts that the family put into reinforcing it with visits to and from a country where the minority language is widely spoken, spending time with other speakers of the language within the community, reading to the children, minority language au-pairs, audio-visual materials, and so on.

All this was especially clear among the families that lived in France or the French–speaking part of Switzerland. As French is a language that enjoys worldwide prestige, there didn't seem to be a lot of support or encouragement towards learning Finnish, which is a much smaller language. In Finland, however, bilingualism is a common phenomenon, encouraged and admired by many, especially if the second language is one of such international standing as French. Even so, the families living in Finland noticed that they too needed to find ways to reinforce their children's French, which was not spoken all around them as Finnish was.

From theory to practice

Once my study was done, I felt relieved. As any 25-year-old would, I naively felt that I had all the answers, and that this was going to be a piece of cake. Our daughter Emma was born in 2001, and we happily set out down the path of raising the first of our bilingual children. During the following years, we realized that we were really just beginning to understand this fascinating phenomenon, and continued reading books and searching for advice to make our daughters' (suddenly there were two!) journeys into bilingualism and biculturalism as pleasant and natural for them as possible. We enjoyed all the literature available on the subject for bilingual families and learned from it.

However, many of the ways to actually put into practice what the experts suggested were found outside the books. They were discovered by talking with other families in similar situations, by trying to be as inventive as possible, and then putting these ideas to the test with the kids (a process of trial and error in itself).

I also noticed over the years that many of the people who asked us for advice about raising bilingual children were looking for simple, straightforward answers and practical tips. It became clear to me that they were interested in the subject, but did not want to spend the time and money on books they felt were too academic or theoretical. With this in mind, I started working on a practical guidebook for parents of multilingual families that would present this how-to information, in a compressed and easy-to-read form, alongside the wisdom and scientific research of the experts. Realizing quite quickly that the word "guidebook" was very challenging (it's difficult to cover and give advice for all situations), I decided to call it an ideabook: a book that is written by one parent for other parents trying to make sense of what the experts say and making it actually work in practice.

I can't take credit for all of the ideas myself. I would particularly like to acknowledge two websites that do great work in promoting multilingualism and multiculturalism: IncultureParent (**incultureparent.com**) and Multilingual Living (**multilingualliving.com**). Not only have these sites been a continuous source of inspiration to me, but with the gracious help of their administrators, I was also able to find and connect with many other multilingual families to ask them about the things that have worked in their multilingual lives.

I would also like to thank the fifty or so multilingual families from around the world that participated in this project by filling out a questionnaire and sharing the best tips from their everyday lives with me. There are as many bilingual situations as there are families and not all ideas presented here will apply to your situation. Neither should they be considered proscriptive. I do hope, though, that you can find ideas to incorporate into what you're already doing.

How to use this book

To avoid confusion, let me explain briefly how this book works. I have tried to base the different chapters and topics on what the experts have written and have summarized the conclusions and advice from the literature in the sections entitled: "Words from the wise". When the information comes from me or other parents, it is either under the headline "View from the front lines" (if you don't have children yet this might not make sense to you, but just you wait) or sometimes "Tried & Tested". This way, you always know who is talking and what is based on scientific research, as well as what stems from the practical experience of real families in real situations. In addition, there are anecdotes at the beginning of each chapter and here and there to illustrate points. For these, I will note my sources wherever possible.

To make the text more readable, I avoid citing scientific references in the text; the expert advice is based on the literature presented in the *References* at the end of the book. Anyone interested in more details concerning my references can contact me at **Annika@be-bilingual.net**. By "experts" I mean linguists and other researchers who have studied and published articles and books on their own research or that of others in their field of study. I emphasize this, as I have sometimes heard people refer to teachers, doctors and other types of professionals as experts. However, unless these experts in their own fields have studied bilingualism, they might not be qualified to give advice in matters related to it.

This book is in two parts: the first is about planning how bilingualism fits into family life and what changes might be necessary according to the goals the family has. In the second part, we focus on how to make this all work - no more theory, just action! At the end of the book you will find a glossary of terms.

Because of our family's personal journey raising French-speaking children in Finland, many of the concrete examples are related to French - our minority language. A website (**be-bilingual.net**) accompanies this book and on that site I invite you, dear reader, to join me in creating a database of materials in many other languages as well. There is also a Facebook page dedicated to this; please join us also there to share your tips and ideas for different languages: **www.facebook.com/bebilingual.net**

Time flies when you have children. What started nearly 15 years ago was a journey to find out how to make sure our own children would become bilingual. Today, as Emma and Sara are 12 and 7 years of age respectively, this is no longer a worry for me. I marvel at the way they are at ease with their two languages and cultures, and I feel that, so far, bilingualism has been a fun and exciting journey for us (while remembering at the same time, that neither of our daughters is a teenager yet!). Our story and situation is only one among many, many different ones. We have friends that are living abroad as expats and change countries every few years, who are dealing with a different aspect of multilingualism. As I'm writing this, we are also expecting a new addition to our extended family through international adoption. This will be a very happy event, a meeting of people that will be very important to each other in the future, but who also, for the moment, don't have a common language.

I've done my best to look for information that is useful in different situations. I hope it will help you, and if it does, I'd love to hear about it! However, the same is also true if it doesn't, and if I have, in your opinion, forgotten something important. I'm very much looking forward to hearing from you.

Part 1 – Planning it out

Chapter 1.   *Bilingualism – what definition and goals are suitable for your family?*

Defining Bilingualism

Many people have a definition of bilingualism that they might strongly feel is the right one. As we shall see, even the linguists can't come up with just one definition although nearly every book I've read on the subject starts with an attempt to find common ground on this very question. The way I see it, there might not be a right or wrong answer, but the most important definition of bilingualism for your family is your own. What exactly does the word mean to you? It's not an unimportant question, as your answer will undoubtedly determine the bilingual goals you have for your family and the priority that it will take in your everyday life.

Words from the wise

The terms "bilingual" and "multilingual" are generally used by linguists as synonyms to refer to a person having two or more languages. As to what having two or more languages actually means, the only consensus seems to be that there is no accepted, general definition to satisfy everyone. The dictionary might define it as simply as "speaking two languages", without being more specific about the skill level, but many writers on the subject are more demanding, although they still do not see eye to eye on the matter.

Even higher-level academic definitions range from requiring fluency in both languages, whenever and however acquired, to claiming that "true bilinguals" have, in addition to this, learned their languages in early childhood, and have native-like spoken and written skills in both. Most would agree, though, that this latter definition would rule out most people, since only a small number among the bilinguals of the world (estimated at about half the global population) have equal fluency and knowledge of both their languages.

The reasons behind this are that bilinguals rarely use their languages for the exact same purposes or situations, so they have different needs for each language. In many of these cases, the language spoken in the daily living environment will become **dominant,** as there is more opportunity to hear and practice it; this is why many experts today suggest that the emphasis should be on language *use* rather than language *skills.* In other words, a bilingual person would be one who uses both (or more) languages daily, even at different degrees of fluency.

View from the front lines

Studying the questionnaires from the parents who took part in my research confirmed that, just like the experts, the parents also have very different views on the definition of bilingualism. Indeed, the definitions I collected were as diverse as the families. Some felt comfortable calling anyone able to communicate in two or more languages a bilingual, many mentioned the word "functional", and for others, bilingualism also included **biliteracy** - being able to read and write in both languages. For some parents, there was a direct connection between bilingualism and biculturalism and a sense of belonging to two cultures. For a minority, bilingualism was the synonym for having native-level fluency in two different languages and being able to take advantage of opportunities afforded to locals in either country.

It's interesting to note that, in most cases, the personal definition of bilingualism that parents used was very closely connected to the goals they mentioned for their family's bilingualism. Many parents also believed that there could be many types and levels of bilingualism, depending on whether the language learning happened in childhood or later in life.

Like the experts, we can all agree to disagree and each have our own definition. For the purpose of this e-book, which is about family bilingualism, I suggest we focus on the type of bilingualism that happens, in various ways and to various degrees of fluency, according to the family's goals, somewhere during childhood. As a language teacher (and learner), I applaud all efforts to learn a language at any point in time, and know that in some cases, language learning later in life gives results that would comply even with the strictest definition of bilingualism. However, having recently attempted to learn Italian I feel quite confident in saying that for most of us adults, we're talking about very different mechanisms here. Anybody with me?

Setting Goals

Emma plays soccer and enjoys it a lot. Among the different girls in her team there are many levels of competence; some of the girls seem to have a talent for the sport that they were born with. However, there's more to the story than meets the eye. Talking with both the parents and the girls, we often see that they have, since an early age, had a lot of instruction and opportunity to practice the sport. This has been a priority within the family and the goals have been set high - in some cases even for the girls to one day, if they so choose, play professionally.

For other families involved with the team, like us, it is enough that the girls get physical exercise and the experience of being a team player. Depending on these different motivations, the families put more or less importance and effort into the development of their children's skills in the sport. The same applies to bilingual development – what is important for your family?

Words from the wise

Researchers talk about multilingual families often setting the bar at the highest level of proficiency, but not planning how this will actually happen, and then being disappointed with the results. Each family is different, and it is important to find out what their personal motivations and goals are, in order to plan the time and language exposure that is needed to achieve them.

Many writers on bilingualism suggest that parents think about the different levels of competence when embarking on the bilingual journey, and set their goals according to what is important to them. The common denominator for the following levels is that generally, the higher the level, the more effort is needed from parents to ensure their children have enough language exposure in different situations in both (or all) languages.

When setting goals for family bilingualism, the families decide if it's important that the children have some or all of the following skills:

1) An understanding of what is said in both languages, but speaking only one of them.

2) An understanding of and participation in the minority language when talking about everyday topics with, for example, the extended family.

3) Oral fluency in both languages.

4) Sufficient fluency in both languages to attend school in either or both (i.e. they speak, read and write in both languages).

As a rule of thumb, experts say that a child needs to be exposed to a language for a minimum of 30% of time spent awake in order to start (and continue) using the language actively. Depending on the child's age, 30% comes to about 25 hours a week, and is a good measure for families when planning realistic family goals.

View from the front lines:

Most Finns are lucky in the sense that they have seen and personally met countless examples of very successful cases of Finnish-Swedish bilingualism, so most people feel that this is a positive thing and relatively **balanced bilingualism** a reachable goal, despite what the experts say about it being a rare phenomenon. At least in the Finnish capital region, it is quite common to meet people who are very competent in both their languages.

What most people don't necessarily realize is that the environment in which children live plays a big part in these positive outcomes. There is great support for both of these languages in the community around us. As both are official languages in Finland, there are countless opportunities to practice both Finnish and Swedish: schooling, hobbies and cultural activities can be chosen in either language. It is very easy to have sufficient exposure in both languages with minimal planning, especially in the greater Helsinki area.

The situation is, however, very different when the bilingual family's second language is one that doesn't exist in the community to such a degree. In such circumstances, achieving similar success for both languages requires a lot more effort and planning to ensure enough exposure to the non-community language. Over the years since I started writing my thesis, I have met dozens of parents who started out with high hopes for their family's bilingualism, but who have been disappointed because they had not realized, from the outset, the amount of effort and planning that would be required to achieve their goal. Many of these families finally settled for a lower level of bilingualism, when in fact a little more planning might have made a big difference to the outcome.

Before defining your goals, here are a few things to consider:

How realistic is it for your child to have at least 25 hours of exposure to the minority language(s) per week?

This might be relatively easy when the children are small and it's easier to control their language environment. I have met many parents of four-year-olds who are convinced that the dominance of the community language will not affect their children's bilingualism.

If this does turn out to be true, then that's great, but most of the time, as children grow, they tend to spend more and more time outside the home at different activities with friends – often in the majority language. Teenagers are a whole different ballgame, I've been told. From the way my preteen acts already, I can imagine there will be a time soon when communication will be a rare occurrence. This is not meant to worry you or put you off bilingualism, but rather to focus your mind on the following important question:

How much time and effort are you personally willing to invest in providing your children with exposure and the possibility to interact in both languages?

We don't usually plan to fail but we sometimes fail to plan. This is not surprising, given the common belief that children are sponges who can simply absorb two languages from their environment. It sounds promising, but as each family's situation is different, it's better to stop first and look at what there is to absorb in the language environment. Sponges only absorb when dipped in water, not thin air or good will. A language can be present in a child's environment if s/he hears it from grandma once a week. While this can be great for the child on many levels, it probably leaves the language sponge pretty dry, and won't realistically produce fluency in the language.

Only you can decide what the right outcome for your family's bilingualism might be, but it's good to know how language exposure works so that you can do the necessary planning. Remember, however, that bilingualism is only one part of your child's development. Be careful not to focus so much on language proficiency that you ignore the importance of harmonious family relationships in the process.

Chapter 2.   ***Why be bilingual? Myths disproved by scientific research***

Around the time I was born, in the mid-seventies, many people were under the impression that bilingualism had negative effects on children's development and intelligence. Behind this were decades of poorly-designed tests that didn't compare like with like, and many of the results of these early studies had more to do with social, rather than language, differences. The tide turned in the sixties, when Canadian scientists showed that bilinguals were actually doing better than monolinguals in some tasks. These positive findings, which have been replicated in many studies since, took a while to reach the general public, and even today, the situation seems confusing to many. Some people still wonder if there is a possible danger in bilingualism, whereas others claim bilingual children to be of superior intelligence.

Words from the wise

The myths that bilingualism causes mental confusion, speech problems, a lowering of the child's intelligence and many more difficulties have been discredited in study after study by scientists since the sixties. Bilingual children have been shown to start speaking within the same time frame and to exhibit a similar pattern of speech development as monolinguals. Bilinguals can suffer from language disorders or learning disabilities in the same way that monolinguals can, but the risks of developing such problems are not higher in bilingual families. Instead, research has found many benefits in being bilingual, especially when both languages are relatively well-developed. While talking about superior intelligence is an exaggeration, regularly using two or more languages seems to enhance brain elasticity and helps bilinguals perform better in some thinking-related tasks.

Furthermore, scientists explain that bilingual children often have more knowledge about the symbolic nature of language (also called **metalinguistic awareness**) than monolinguals of the same age. Having two or more languages, the bilingual children often start to understand the nature of language and how it works earlier. They can think of their languages abstractly, because they know that the same object or idea can be referred to with two (or more) different words. They might also realize, at a conscious level early on, how changes in phrasing, word order, or verb tense can change the meaning of what is said.

What does this mean in practice? Scientists claim that having this knowledge about language itself and its functions is the foundation of learning to read and write, and that bilingual children are often ready to do so earlier. Experts often link this ability to think abstractly to academic success and creativity. Another key here is that children who realize that they have different languages at their disposal need to choose the one that the person they're speaking with also speaks. While doing this, they are focusing their attention on one thing and ignoring what is not essential (in other words, the language that is useless in this situation), which also seems to make bilinguals better problem solvers, as they can concentrate on the problem at hand despite distractions. Using several languages regularly seems to be very beneficial for the brain, and there is evidence that it might even increase the density of the brain's grey matter. The good news for all bilinguals is that recent studies have shown bilingualism to be better than any drug in delaying the onset of Alzheimer's disease.

Scientists believe that the positive effects on the brain increase as proficiency does. However, research is currently being carried out to further study the threshold hypothesis to identify the level of proficiency in both languages that is necessary to reap the cognitive benefits of bilingualism. Some studies have already shown that even a less-developed second language can bring with it thinking advantages if the first language is well-developed at an age-appropriate level. In addition to this, there are, of course, many other advantages to even just understanding another language. Passive knowledge can be activated in the right situation when the child has the need and desire to speak a language with a lot less effort than learning a language from scratch.

Whether passive or active in their language use, children can also benefit from bilingualism in many other ways that can't be similarly measured. It can serve as a channel to the extended family and provide access to the children's cultural heritage on each parent's side. Moreover, speaking and understanding several languages helps children become more open towards different cultures and contributes to both the tolerance and the appreciation of difference.

View from the front lines

I learned about the thinking-related benefits connected with bilingualism when I wrote my thesis on the subject. Gilles and I had, however, made the decision to raise our children bilingually long before that. We instinctively wanted our children to get to experience both their cultures from the inside and interact naturally with family members from both sides. As they have grown, the most important rewards have been the strong and natural ties that they have been able to form with their French relatives, as there is no language barrier. The cognitive advantage is a plus, but not what is most important to us.

However, it's good to talk about the other benefits too, however, as old myths die hard. We saw this recently with an article published in an online newspaper that warned parents against a language disorder brought on by learning several languages at the same time. The article was quickly distributed across social media as alarmed parents posted it as a well-meaning "warning" to other parents in the same situation as themselves. How many actually read the article before passing it on is unknown, but what many people probably retained from it was that multilingualism is in some way dangerous to their children's language development. It was, however, basically the same myth that existed several decades ago, and one which multiple studies have since proved wrong.

In the two cases the article discussed, both families had problems on many levels. The pre-school girl and the first grade boy were described as reluctant to speak the languages and struggling to learn them. They were also showing symptoms of stress and loss of appetite. Both cases took place in Asia, where the parents, having heard of the multiple benefits of bilingualism, had hoped to transform their children into language prodigies by enrolling them in language classes in three different foreign languages at the same time. Surprised after a while that the experiment wasn't going smoothly and producing the language geniuses they had hoped, the parents came to the conclusion that the problem was in learning several languages at the same time. As many comments on the article by parents of multilingual families showed, the outcome of the "experiment" was not surprising to them.

These particular cases are a far cry from the circumstances under which experts claim children are capable of acquiring up to five languages simultaneously. The literature on bilingualism is full of examples of children mastering four and, sometimes, even more languages (to various degrees of fluency, depending on the exposure they have to those languages), and doing so with pleasure when they feel an actual need and desire to learn and use their language skills with people they want to communicate with. Both parents might speak different languages with the child, the grandma or nanny might use a third one, and a fourth one could be learned at school or in the community. This is why, when referring to bilingual children, the word *acquisition* is often used instead of the word *learning*. They are not consciously learning, but acquiring the necessary skills as they go about discovering the world through play and meaningful communication. It is in this natural setting, where there is no pressure to perform and the children are not afraid of making mistakes (just eager to communicate!), that the special abilities they have are harnessed, rather than through formal teaching in a classroom.

Chapter 3.   *Bilingualism from birth or later?*

Recently, I visited friends who had just had their first child. The parents come from different countries and speak different native languages as well as the language they speak with each other, making a total of three languages in their household altogether.. My friends, knowing my fascination with the subject, asked me for my opinion about their situation: should they introduce both their native languages immediately or wait until one language is firmly in place? Knowing that neither of them speaks the native language of the other, I just smiled and asked which one of them would be willing not to speak to their child for the first few years.

Words from the wise

The situation might not always be as clear cut as that above. The parents might each speak both languages and wonder whether they should start by using just one of the languages they have in common, and have one parent switch to another language later when the child has learned the first one. The scientific terms for these two different methods are **Simultaneous Bilingualism** (when the languages are both learned during the first three or four years) and **Successive Bilingualism** (when the second language is learned after the first one is already in place). According to the experts, both ways can be successful from a linguistic point of view. In simultaneous bilingualism, the child is actually learning both languages in the same way as a monolingual child learns his or her mother tongue. Instead of having one first language, he or she has two: one from each parent.

As for successive bilingualism, a child that has a solid first language can transfer these skills to the second language. He or she wouldn't start by learning just words as with the first language, but would rapidly proceed to expressing his or her needs with phrases. Many experts argue that this might be especially beneficial if both parents spoke the non-community language at home and delayed the introduction of the community language, which easily becomes dominant, until around preschool age. On the contrary, starting with the majority language and not introducing the non-community language until later might mean giving up on it altogether. It is very difficult to change a language within a family once a pattern has been established, and the child might not feel the need to speak in a new language (that other people in the community don't speak) to a parent that s/he has so far been able to talk to in the (easier) community language.

There seems to be an age at which the brain loses some of its language learning capability, or at least this ability changes. Scientists don't agree on when this happens; some claim it's as early as six years of age, whereas others stretch it out to somewhere in early puberty. After this elusive threshold, the brain has been trained to focus on a certain set of sounds – in other words, those of the mother tongue(s). From then on, the child's ear will filter all the sounds through the ones s/he recognizes because they are present in the native language(s), making it more difficult to learn native-like pronunciation. The experts claim that this is the reason why most adult language learners have foreign accents.

Young children also have the advantage that the language spoken to them is usually easier and expectations from the community are lower. A further plus is that they are also learning many other things through trial and error, and are therefore not afraid of making mistakes. They are used to it being a part of learning and don't really care whether they make mistakes or not – as long as the message gets across!

View from the front lines

Many parents agree that changing the language in the family can be difficult for both sides and tend to recommend that, when introducing another language, especially the minority one, it is a case of "the earlier the better". Even at the age of three, children already understand that they can speak to the parent in the community language, if that's the one they've been using until then, and can resist the introduction of a new language.

This became very clear to me when I spoke to a Swedish friend about her situation. She lived in the U.S. and spoke English to her three- and five-year-old sons because, at the time of their birth, she hadn't really planned for bilingualism, and it felt easy to speak English – just like everyone else around the baby. However, having read about the benefits of bilingualism, she started to regret this decision. Encouraged by the research that showed that it wasn't yet too late, she asked for my advice.

Together, we made an action plan that first included finding other Swedes in her area. A quick Google search helped us locate SWEA, an international organization for Swedish speakers, and she contacted them to find more local Swedish connections. This would be useful to help her keep up the motivation to speak the language, and, eventually, to help her sons to meet other Swedish-speaking children. Other possibilities I suggested that she look into were materials like books and DVDs, the use of Swedish-speaking babysitters from time to time, and maybe even an au pair to make the switch into Swedish more natural. I noticed that her enthusiasm was starting to wane and that it was all beginning to feel like a lot of work to her. Add in some resistance from the children (which was to be expected), and I wasn't too surprised that a few months later, she told me that she had given up on the project. She had felt frustrated with the children not understanding her and had found herself falling back into English to make it easier on herself and them. She told me she really regretted not having been more disciplined with herself and not having spoken Swedish to them from birth.

This is not meant to discourage those starting bilingualism later on – anytime is better than never! It's just good to be forewarned that some effort on the part of the parent and resistance from the children will probably be involved. Some ideas that can apply here will also be presented in Chapter 5, which is about raising children using a non-native language. As for those who are planning, expecting, or have small babies, the consensus from parents seems to be to start early, if possible, in order to make it easier for yourself and the whole family.

Chapter 4.   *Your language approach – what is right for your family?*

Most multilingual families usually decide at some point how their languages are organized within the family: who speaks which language to whom and when. This may be a conscious decision, or it might just happen by doing what feels natural. This language arrangement can be called a strategy, a system, or a rule; personally, I like the word "approach". There is no magic formula or only one right approach - the right one is the one that suits your family.

Words from the wise

There is no authority that defines the languages a family must use. Friends, relatives and people in positions of authority, like teachers and doctors, may have opinions on the subject, which we either take into account or ignore. Ultimately, it is the family that decides the language pattern in their own home.

While experts acknowledge that, to some degree, children can learn another language in very disorganized conditions, most recommend that there should be at least some guidelines about who speaks which language in order for the children to become fluent speakers. Any approach is often as successful as the parents are consistent in using it. Writers on the subject suggest that the following questions might be useful for parents when planning the language scheme of the family:

- Which languages are important for the family to keep alive (for heritage or practical reasons)?

- Which languages are each parent most comfortable using?

- Which approach would help the two or more desired languages develop most equally in the family's specific situation?

- Which approach will ensure the long-term development of both (or more) languages?

Whatever approach you choose, the experts reassure bilingual families that the decision is not set in stone: circumstances in life change, and may call for adjustments to or movement in another direction from the first approach you choose. Your approach forms the foundation for language use in the family, but won't determine everything, and nor is it likely to be enough to ensure family bilingualism. The more the community is monolingual, the more the non-community language will need to be reinforced.

One interesting thing the literature points out is that the parents are not the only ones controlling the language scene at home. As children grow, they have more and more influence over this, and can have personal preferences for language use. Through school, friends and the language the siblings decide to use among themselves (without asking the parents if it's part of the family approach), the language balance in the family may shift.

There are as many approaches as there are families, but linguists have defined three main ones with infinite variations: *The one-parent-one-language* approach, *the minority language at home* approach, and the *mixed language* approach.

Approach A: OPOL – connecting the language to the person

When Emma was born, Gilles and I spoke to her in our native languages, French and Finnish respectively. This not only felt the most natural to us, but was also *the* approach that was considered to produce the best results at the time. Even if the presence of both languages at home meant that extra time and effort needed to be put into French, Emma separated her languages from the start and associated each language with the right person – she was a textbook example. Just before her second birthday, she spent some time alone with her French grandparents and at some point asked for something in Finnish. When her puzzled grandparents didn't understand her, she got very upset. Finally, her grandmother thought of asking: "But how does daddy say it?" Gilles' mother later told us that she saw the realization dawn on the child as Emma stopped crying and said the words again, this time in French. Ten years later, Grandma still tells this story in praise of OPOL.

Words from the wise

At the time I was writing my thesis in the late nineties, most linguists recommended the *one-parent-one-language approach* (often abbreviated to OPOL) almost unconditionally. It was considered *the* most natural way of creating bilingualism in a multilingual family, since both parents could form a relationship with the child in their own native languages. There were no complicated rules: the language was naturally associated with the person who used it, as long as the parents were consistent in their habits and didn't mix the two languages. Consistency was easy to maintain, as both the other parent and the children observed the agreed language use.

Even today, experts find many advantages in OPOL as an effective strategy for children to acquire two languages from birth, and claim that when used consistently, it might reduce the tendency of the children to mix those languages. It seems to help set language boundaries and avoid language chaos within the family. Part of its success might be that this approach helps the children's two cultures live harmoniously in the same household, and contributes to creating emotional links with each language. Many believe that OPOL is most successful when the family is part of a minority language community, as it helps ensure the child has sufficient input in both languages.

Since the nineties, however, linguists have also found an increasing number of drawbacks to the OPOL approach, with the main ones being the amount of work and effort needed to keep children motivated and the difficulty in providing enough exposure to the minority language for them to be able to speak it. It is rare that each parent spends the same amount of time with their children, so the language of the community becomes dominant very easily. Linguists seem to agree that without considerable effort put into reinforcing the minority language, the children in OPOL families have a high probability of, in time, becoming receptive bilinguals who understand the minority language but prefer to speak the community language. Many suggest that to help give more equality to the two languages, the parents should, if they can, use the minority language between themselves.

View from the front lines

Many parents who use the *one-parent-one-language* approach say that they didn't consciously decide to do so, but that it had just felt natural for each parent to use his or her native language with the child. For many, the idea of speaking another language to their child had been either impossible because of a lack of language skills, or rather, it simply hadn't felt right. Several respondents to the questionnaire claimed that they felt better able to bond with the baby in the language their own mother had used with them. It often seemed to be the approach adopted by many who had either done what had felt natural without giving it much thought (in terms of providing the children with equal exposure to both languages), or who lived in communities where support for the minority language was easily accessible. There are still many who feel that it is the best strategy, and the only imaginable one in their family's situation.

One inconvenience that keeps being mentioned, even by the proponents of this approach, is that in families where one of the parents doesn't understand the language of the other, each sticking to one's own language tends to isolate one or both parents from conversations with the children. To be more socially sensitive, many call themselves "OPOLish" and change to the majority (or other mutual) language for the purposes of connecting the family when together, or to be polite when around monolingual friends or relatives. Many consider it rude to speak to children in a language not understood by others, and tiresome and tedious to constantly translate everything back and forth.

If one thinks only of language acquisition, it is true that it can be difficult to require the children to use the minority language when alone with the parent, when at other times they are allowed to use the majority language. Still, some feel that strict use of OPOL, even in the presence of those who don't understand, is putting the achievement of bilingualism ahead of the one thing it is supposed to promote: having a means of communication and understanding. Some even go so far as to say that it may set a bad example to the children, who can later use it as a tool to manipulate parents or other people by leaving them out of conversations.

Many families with children who go to school claim that, in many cases, the OPOL strategy, especially if it's a strict one, is a phase. Many have noticed that once the patterns of communication had been established and the children were comfortable using both languages, the language strategy in the family became more relaxed.

Parents feel that OPOL can be a good choice if one or more of the following variables is true:

- You are a mixed-language couple, and you both feel strongly about speaking your own language to your child.

- You are a fluent speaker of a foreign language and want to speak to your child in that language.

- You live in a community where you have good support for the minority language.

- Your minority language is one that has a certain prestige in your country of residence.

- One of the spouses (or both) doesn't speak the language of the other (but hopefully understands it, and is either willing to make an effort to acquire at least a passive knowledge of the language or alternatively, doesn't mind not understanding every word that is said).

- Both parents speak a (different) non-community language.

- You are willing to invest time and effort into reinforcing the minority language (in ways we will look at in this book).

- The family is likely to travel regularly to the country where the minority language is spoken.

- The person speaking the minority language is the main caretaker of the children, or has time to spend with them.

- Another person outside the immediate family can serve as a regular language model for your child (in which case the P in OPOL stands for person, not parent).

Approach B: Minority language at home – linking the language to a place or a group of people

The first time my daughter casually asked me to pass her the milk in French, I chuckled. I was so used to her always speaking another language to me, that it felt surreal. She didn't notice my reaction, as she was busy explaining something to her sister, also in French. The conversation at the dinner table flowed in all directions in French, just as it had done in a mixture of French and Finnish before. We were all fluent in both, and it really didn't matter anymore which language we spoke together. So, I figured, why not consciously use our minority language to give it an extra boost?

Words from the wise

A family may decide to speak only the minority language with its members or do so only when the family is at home together. In the latter case, the language choice would be linked to the place instead of the people, as the same people would speak a different language together, depending on the location.

What was still considered by many experts to be artificial in the nineties has since gained popularity, to the point that it is today the approach that many linguists recommend. Its success is based on studies that show that everyone using the same language in the home might increase the chances of success in transmitting both languages by as much as 20 percent, compared to using both languages at home. Among the families that I interviewed for my thesis, only one family had adopted this strategy, and all family members spoke the non-community language at home. The Finnish mother was fluent in French, and this family had certainly experienced many of the positive effects referred to by the experts: while Finnish (the community language) was left outside the home, the children spoke French with each other, even when left alone.

The *one-language-one-environment* strategy is recommended by many experts equally to families in which both parents are native speakers of the minority language, as well as to those in which it is a non-native language for one of the parents. This way, the children have more exposure to the language, which is not interrupted by one of the family members speaking the majority language. This increased exposure not only means that there are more people speaking the language to the child, but also that there are more opportunities for him or her to communicate in that language and practice their language skills. The home becomes a haven for the minority language that leaves its majority counterpart outside – at least to some extent.

One of the few inconveniences that the experts mention is that even with this approach, the language of the external environment can easily become dominant once the child goes to school or attends other activities in the majority language. To counteract this, many experts suggest (although some parents may think it radical) that it might be a good idea not to expose the child to the community language at all until preschool or kindergarten. Parents may worry about their child being at a disadvantage compared to the monolingual children in the community, but experts say that this has not been found to be a problem in any studies. The children are eager and motivated to learn the language of their classmates, and will generally reach the same level very quickly.

Depending on the family, some parents will speak the home language with their children at all times, but some choose to switch to the majority language when they're out in the community or among monolingual speakers. The experts don't see a problem with either, keeping in mind that just as for OPOL, children might not see a reason not to speak the majority language with their parents and siblings at home too, since it is acceptable at other times. Some experts claim that this strategy (sometimes abbreviated to mL@H) is easy and beneficial to apply, especially when the children are younger, and that it boosts the early acquisition and appreciation of the minority language before community influences, particularly school and friends, become stronger.

View from the front lines

Having been a strict advocate of OPOL, I was at first surprised and somewhat skeptical to read about the recent evidence in favor of this approach, which seemed to say that our family might be better off, at least linguistically, if I spoke French, my non-native language, to my children. Even if I had always known that our children would learn Finnish from the community no matter what I did, it had been important to me that they learn *my* Finnish. I could not help but notice, however, that as our children grew, they were spending more and more time at activities and with friends in the community language (which, by the way, was not that different from *my* Finnish).

In the blogosphere, on websites like Multilingual Living or Inculture Parent, and through books on the subject, I made contact with a great number of people who were using the mL@H approach. Some had started right away when their children were born and some had adopted the approach later. Even if I usually take everything on the Internet with a grain of salt, I had to admit that there were many positive testimonials on behalf of this approach. I will explain in more depth in Chapter 11 how I examined our situation and the amount of French the girls were exposed to daily, and decided, with Gilles' compliance, to try and gradually move into speaking French with the girls when we were all together. To cut a long story short, it wasn't that difficult, and with a few minor exceptions, our family relationship also worked just fine in French.

In the replies I received from fellow parents, I noticed that many others had also implemented a partly OPOL / partly mL@H approach in the house. For many who, like myself, were not ready to move entirely into the other language, adopting the common language as soon as the other parent walked in the door was a convenient language boundary. In our case, there was some initial resistance from the girls: they didn't mind replying in French, but continued to address me in Finnish. However, a few weeks into the experiment, an interesting thing happened. When the whole family was at home, but not doing something together, the girls started speaking French more spontaneously to each other. They still spoke less of it to me, but it seemed as if the French I was using had tilted the language balance towards French in our house.

Parents feel that mL@H can be a good choice if one or more of the following variables is true:

- Both parents share a native language that is different to the community language.

- The minority language is not one that enjoys international prestige like English or French.

- You live in a place where there is little support or few resources for the minority language and you feel very strongly about your children receiving maximum exposure to that language.

- The parent who is the native speaker of the minority language doesn't have a lot of time to spend with the children or is often away from home.

- Both parents feel proficient enough and natural about speaking the home language, even if it's not necessarily the native language of one (or both) of them. If you feel uneasy about your language skills but would still like to do it, don't be worried. There is a lot of evidence that shows you can still introduce a non-native language to your child. Do, however, read Chapter 5, which is about raising children using a non-native language, for some important points to consider.

Approach C: Time and Space or mixing it up

On our trip to Morocco last year, we witnessed an interesting language phenomenon. The people we met, who spoke French to us foreigners, communicated with each other in a mixture of Arabic and French. Our children were fascinated by this and tried to follow the conversations based on the French phrases and words that they could hear intertwined with the Arabic. What to us was a fun game was to them a way of life. Both languages were present in the community, and mixing them together was considered the norm.

Words from the wise

Like the place-bound mL@H, there are other ways to set language boundaries around places, or situations, rather than people. This can also be called the *time and space* approach. Some people use a different language at mealtimes, on certain days of the week, or when doing specific activities (for example, at football practice or during family outings).

MLP (*mixed language policy*) takes this even further and sets language boundaries around topics or situations. The people using this approach might employ one language to talk about school and another to discuss an event. Sometimes there are no boundaries at all, but both or even more languages form a joyous mix in all utterances. This is a very common approach in communities in many Asian countries (and could be seen in the earlier example from north Africa), where the whole community may be multilingual and mixing languages makes sense, as everyone is used to it and understands everything that is being said.

Some argue that whichever approach parents choose, even one where language input is quite arbitrary, children with normal language ability will probably achieve some competence anyway. Linguists don't, however, generally recommend these approaches for families that are committed to having their children achieve a higher level of proficiency in the non-community language(s), as these strategies don't tend to make any effort to support the minority language.

View from the front lines

A time or place-bound approach might work for families in which a non-native parent wants to use both the community language and the non-community language with their children. This would enable the setting of clear boundaries concerning the use of the minority language, meaning the children would not get confused. Read on in order to discover more about this subject and how, in this case, it is important to supplement this exposure to the language with other speakers or language sources.

At the end of the day, many parents suggest that other parents should choose what feels natural based on the priority and goals that each family has for bilingualism. Whichever of these approaches your family decides to adopt, you will find practical tips and ideas to help you in Part 2 of this book.

Chapter 5. *Raising bilingual children in a non-native language*

My friend Jon is a Finn who speaks English to his three children. English is not his mother tongue, but having lived abroad, and the fact that he's been connected with the language in one way or another for most of his life, most people can't tell that he's not a native speaker. There are similar cases and success stories all around the world. I could have personally made the same choice, having lived in France, studied French at university, and spoken it with my husband and many others on a daily basis for years. Yet the pull of the native language was very strong for me. I had not firmly decided to use another language before her arrival, so when little Emma was put in my arms for the very first time, only Finnish words poured out alongside my tears of joy.

Words from the wise

A lot of opinions exist about speaking to your child in a language other than your native one, and a great number of them are not very positive. Feeling myself very strongly about speaking to my own children in my native language (I felt I was passing on not only language or words, but a lifetime of cultural references and memories), I might have been part of the club of critics at one point: opinionated, but uninformed. Yet the literature on the subject is full of success stories about non-native parents raising their children bilingually.

Some have chosen OPOL (approach A) to do it, while some do it alongside their native-speaking spouse to create a home enveloped in the minority language. In some cases, this mL@H environment (approach B), is created by two non-native speakers who leave it to the environment to teach the majority language to their children. Many of them face criticism for this, but the experts claim that it can be a very good strategy if all the pieces of the puzzle are in place. The same laws about exposure to each language also apply to non-native speakers. If the parent(s) uses the native language alongside the non-native one, particular effort may be needed for the children to feel a need to speak the minority language.

Many parents, worried about and critical of their own language skills, might be afraid of making mistakes that their children will copy. While the experts understandably say that parents shouldn't be bad language models to their children, most don't see it as problematic for parents to make mistakes as long as the children also have access to native speakers in that language, in one way or another. This way, the parental linguistic role would not only be a language model, but also a language partner who provides interaction in that language for the child. This interaction makes the child an active participant in the conversation instead of a passive listener.

View from the front lines

There are many reasons why parents might raise their children using a non-native language. Some want to transmit a language that is important to them because they have a special connection with it or the culture it represents. Others want their children to benefit from the advantages bilingualism has for children, be it on a cognitive, social or – later in life – economic level. Some even feel that their native language doesn't sound right to them. Ultimately, this is something that each parent must decide for themselves.

Jane Merrill, the American author of a book about raising her twins in French, her non-native second language, talks about her choice as something very natural: "Bilingual child-rearing is like breast-feeding: it is giving a child a tender gift. It costs you nothing and fits in perfectly with everyday life." She also says, as many other parents in the same situation have discovered, that any initial awkwardness caused by speaking a non-native language quickly fades and a few months later, it would have felt strange to use any other language.

When deciding to speak a non-native language to your child from birth:

- **Plan well:** planning is key. Unless you make a firm decision to do it before your child is born, chances are you won't. This is true for most bilingual families, but especially so when it is not your native language.

- **Decide your language strategy and make sure your spouse is on board!** If you want to speak both your native and non-native language to your child, set clear boundaries around certain activities that you always do in one language (knowing that there are experts who suggest that it may be better to have just one language per person during the first years to avoid confusion).

- **Look for families that are either doing what you are doing in the same language or, better yet, native-speaking families.** This will be a great support, and this type of exposure can also act as a language model for you and your child (baby talk or words for baby-related items are rarely taught at university or in language classes). Also consult parenting forums and websites in your non-native language. Join child-related social-networking groups in your minority language.

- **Take a careful and objective look at your language skills** and commit to improving or maintaining your spoken and written abilities by taking language classes, finding language partners (e.g. **The Mixxer** on Skype), and getting to know people who speak that language. Choose audio programs for the car, light fiction, movies and newspapers in your non-native language. Make that language the default for computer and TV settings.

- **Get as much extra support as you can.** You probably won't get much encouragement or understanding from the environment. Instead, find the support you need on forums like the one on the Multilingual Living website (**multilingualliving.com/forum**), dedicated Facebook groups, and from others who understand why you're doing what you're doing.

- **Don't be intimidated by people** asking you where you're from and having to explain why you speak in a non-native language to your child. Just tell them that you're locals, but that you are, for example, a Spanish-speaking family.

When deciding to speak a non-native language to an older child:

Many of the previous ones apply, but here are a few more ideas that might be useful in this particular situation:

- **Include your older children in the decision**. Ease them into it by introducing the language step-by-step. How about starting with songs and games in that language? Make learning a new word every day into a fun activity that you can build on.

- **Use a third person**. Parents report good results from introducing the language to older children first through a babysitter or an au pair, and then adopting it more at home little by little. This way your children can grow accustomed to the new language and the fact that you are now speaking a different language than the one that they're used to. It would be easy to switch to that language when claiming that the au pair doesn't understand the community language.

- **Try to make speaking the language fun and useful** for your children by organizing play dates with other children who speak that language (more ideas on how to do this later).

- **If possible, plan a trip to the country where the language is spoken**. This can work as a great motivator before the trip, as you can all learn some of the language to use and enjoy it to the full on a future holiday!

Monolingual parents raising a bilingual child

When Emma was about eight, she was fluent and literate in both her native languages, and then I wanted to introduce her to English, which her friends who attended a monolingual Finnish school started learning at her age. She participated in a three-day English *immersion* camp at the beginning of the summer vacation, and we continued English language learning together in a very relaxed manner with flash cards, word-of-the-day games, and role playing. The main motivator for her was a trip to England that she and I would take the year after. I built up the trip (to the point where I got worried about not being able to deliver!) and told her there would be ice cream and other fun stuff, as long as she would ask for it in English. English was "our thing" together and the three-night trip to Manchester was a great success. Today Sara, at age six, is attending weekly immersion classes in English and tells everyone that she, too, will be going to England together with mommy once she can speak to the people there.

Many of the suggestions in this chapter also work when parents would like their children to learn another language, but either don't want to or can't speak that language themselves. Many parents have found it useful, when possible, to enroll their children in an immersion program (school, kindergarten, Saturday school) in the foreign language. In the French-Finnish school, our children have many friends whose parents don't speak French. To help their children with their schoolwork, many have au pairs or hire private tutors when necessary, and the children are doing very well. Some have even arranged for their children to do their homework with classmates whose parents are native French speakers. This arrangement seems to suit everyone: both sets of parents are happy, because the homework gets done correctly, and for the children, it's more fun to do it together.

There is another way for children to learn a foreign language in a monolingual home. More and more people today have the opportunity to relocate to another country for work reasons, and they often bring the whole family along. When people in the host country speak a different language than the family, the relocation presents, along with some challenges, a great opportunity for language learning.

Chapter 6.   *Families in different multilingual situations*

Not all bilingual families have parents that speak different languages. Children (as well as parents) can learn another (or a third) language when the family is relocated abroad for work or other reasons. Through adoption, children often have to learn a new language, in addition to getting to know a new family and environment. Sometimes families have more than two languages, and sometimes only one parent. Let's briefly take a look at these different situations and the ideas and advice that literature, as well as first-hand experience from parents, provides.

Expats

Words from the wise

When a family with children is relocated to another country, one of their first decisions, often based on the estimated length of their stay, is the degree to which they wish to integrate into their new society, and learn the local language. This, in turn, determines whether their children will attend a local school or an international one. Sometimes, whichever option they choose, the language will be different from the home language(s).

Literature on bilingualism doesn't offer many concrete ideas for expatriate families in this situation. However, it does suggest, understandably enough, that up to the age of seven, it is easier for children to learn the host country's language, playing with friends or in the more structured setting of kindergarten. For families with young children, there will usually be few problems, linguistically speaking, if their children enter the local school system from elementary level. At this age, the language used is simpler and there are a lot of possibilities for interaction with other children in the classroom. After this, and especially during the teenage years, it is no longer sufficient to acquire simple conversational proficiency; a different level of language aptitude is necessary when facing a school curriculum, which probably differs from the home in more ways than just language. At this age, there are also self-confidence issues that might make it more difficult to integrate and get to know other people when arriving as an outsider.

Whereas conversational fluency can be reached in a matter of months, the experts believe that academic proficiency takes school-age children between five and seven years to attain. To help the process along, many parents in this situation ask themselves if they should also switch to speaking the new community / school language at home. Most experts agree that this is very rarely a good solution. It is a big enough change for your children to have left home, friends and extended family behind, so many writers suggest that your new home should, in this case, be a place where they can relax and express themselves in the way that is most natural to them. A solid foundation in the home language(s) also helps transfer these skills to the new language.

Ideas from the front lines

The advice a family needs when relocating can be very different, depending on the length of their stay (some change location every few years), how many languages the children already speak, and if schooling is available in any of these languages. Here are a few ideas from parents about some important things to consider when designing your expatriate language arrangement:

- **Determine the languages that are important for the family to keep for heritage reasons,** and for communicating with family members back home. If there is only one such language, would it be possible to keep this language as the home language, and learn another one outside the home? If each parent speaks a different language and there is a third one in the community, read on for more about trilingual children.

- **Evaluate how long you will be staying in the country,** and what the concrete possibilities and value are in keeping up the new language after you leave. Many parents have reported that they initially thought they would only be staying for a short time, but ended up staying for years – and regretted that they didn't expose the children to the language of the community.

- **Consider integrating especially smaller children into a local school,** if there is a possibility that you will stay for a longer time. Do, however, give them time to learn the basics of the language first in a safe environment. An expat family we know experienced a case of selective mutism after they enrolled their three-year-old daughter in a French-speaking school immediately upon arrival in Belgium. Her Finnish language skills had just started to blossom, and all of a sudden she found herself in an environment where she couldn't make herself understood. She chose not to speak a word of French until the family hired a lovely older lady to take care of the children in their own home. The mother of the family told me that she wished they had started by doing this or even by exposing their children to the language before relocation. Expat parents seem to agree with the experts, and recommend that the home language(s) should stay the same, so look for solutions other than you adopting the new language at home. For example, get a babysitter or an au-pair who speaks the language before you relocate.

- **Look for a private tutor in the language for older children.** It can be helpful to do this both before relocation and upon arrival to help them integrate successfully into the local school system. Your new city may also offer preparatory classes that your children can attend for several months to learn the language before entering a local school. Find out more from your embassy and local expat networks. You could also consider arriving several months before the school year starts (for example, during the summer) and getting to know some of the families and children that will be in the same school. This way, your children will be able to practice and get the basics of the language, and they will already know people when school starts.

- **Take into consideration what the school in the home country expects** upon your return when making decisions about schooling. If it's very difficult to meet these expectations, consider part- or full-time home-schooling in your language(s), and learning the community language to the desired extent outside the home. In any case, going over homework in your home language will help both in consolidating the subject matter being learned, and skills in the new language.

- **Continue to support the home language.** If you end up staying for many years, and your children are speaking another language outside the home, it is important to read on about reinforcing the minority language(s), which your home language(s) will probably become. Other expats in your situation in the same area can be a great source of advice and help keep your heritage language(s) alive for your children. You may not want to associate with the "expat crowd" as a few parents put it, but for the sake of your children's language skills, looking for a few like-minded countrymen might not hurt. Here are a few ideas on where to find them:

- **meetup.com**
- **expat-blog.com**
- **internations.org**
- **your location's expat FB page** or **other expat groups in your city** (google them in English and in your minority language as both might yield results).

International Adoption

Words from the wise

A lot of information is available about adopting a child from another country, but very little of this deals with the language issues involved. Most of what has been written is about acquiring the new language, and not about maintaining the old one in the process.

Most of the information that can be found online regarding adoption is not very positive about multilingualism. It states that the child will usually lose his or her native tongue in a matter of months and puts emphasis on learning the new language as quickly as possible to help the child integrate. The message is, sometimes even in these exact words, that "bilingualism and international adoption are not compatible". Maintaining ties with the past and, for example, meeting people from the child's native country (to preserve the heritage language), are thought to possibly create problems and attachment issues, and so hinder bonding with the adoptive family and positive identification with the child's new country. It would seem that many of these opinions consider mainly what is easiest for the parents, not necessarily in the best interest of the adopted child in the long term.

A few experts on bilingualism, such as Colin Baker, author of *A Parents' and Teachers' Guide to Bilingualism*, see things differently. While Mr. Baker agrees that there are many things to take into consideration, such as the child's age, background, and personal preferences, situations available for language exposure, and so on, he encourages the parents to maintain the child's first language if at all possible. Instead of seeing this as a cause of problems, he claims that the child's self-esteem can benefit from an acknowledgment of identity and origin instead of ignoring it as something of no value. Even a passive understanding of the heritage language can be valuable in the future, as it can be activated and built on. The child might very well wish to improve native language ability at a later stage, although the most important thing for now might be to integrate into the mainstream culture with same-age peers.

Research also shows other benefits to retaining the child's first language. Studies show that a complete loss of the native language before the new one has had time to develop sufficiently to communicate impacts negatively on the child's cognitive development. Many adopted children already suffer from language delays and learning disabilities, and losing the first language before gaining another one could add to this, and make it difficult for the child to learn their new language to a deeper level than simple conversational fluency.

View from the frontlines

This issue is very close to my heart, as we are expecting a new member in our extended family through international adoption. So far, we know nearly nothing about the person we so dearly await: not even gender, nor age. However, the one thing we do know is the country the child will come from, and based on this, we can make an educated guess that he or she will not have the same native language as the adoptive parents.

Concerned with the lack of information, and the poor quality of some that I did find online, I looked further and found a very useful website called linguistlist.org. Through their service "Ask a Linguist", I posted a question about our situation and was pleasantly surprised to receive several very supportive and encouraging answers, one of which came from the well-known linguist, author, and multilingual mother of an equally multilingual family, Madalena Cruz-Ferreira. She really went out of her way to help me understand the issue and what the best way to approach the situation would be.

It's very inspiring to hear from an expert with such a practical outlook on things as Madalena, who wrote to me about her frustration over the fact that so many people consider "integration" to mean being monolingual, and "diversity" to be, by definition, a negative thing. "In the real world," she wrote, "people bond with several cultures and several languages. A child should not be deprived of choices."

Here are a few of her thoughts and ideas for parents planning international adoption:

- **Understand the options**. Integration doesn't have to mean your child should be monolingual or deprived of choices.

- **Learn a bit of your new child's native language beforehand** as an exciting way to get a window into his or her culture. It's also a foolproof way to show your child that you care, and understand what he or she is, and will be, going through.

- **Look for networks or interest groups** concerning the community that your child comes from. Embassies, cultural centers, and women's associations might all be helpful here. Through these, find other children which your child can befriend that speak his or her native language. Children should be able to talk with other children about things that interest them. The same thing is good for learning the new home language. However, stick to one little friend at a time with your child – or else the fluent speakers will talk mostly to one another!

- **Find other resources like books, magazines and videos** in the native language and about the native country. It might be a good idea to look for these during the trip over to bring your child home.

Of course, each adoption case is different, and there is no foolproof recipe. It might also be that your family is already bilingual and you are wondering whether or not to introduce both languages to your adopted child right away. Becky Morales from **kidworldcitizen.com** is a great example of making this work. Having adopted two children from two different countries into their already bilingual home, she and her husband not only spoke their respective native languages with their children straight away, but also made a great effort to retain the children's original cultures. Here are a few of her very practical suggestions to adoptive families:

- **Look for international students and cultural groups at local universities**. It is a great cultural exchange because the students can learn about their host families while the family can learn about their child's birth culture and language.

- **Get a babysitter or nanny who speaks the child's language**. The child should also be around native speakers, and if the parents are not, a babysitter is a great addition.

- **Attend churches or places of worship and cultural centers**. Immigrants often congregate with fellow citizens of their home country to celebrate religious festivals, which is a great place for your kids to play and meet other kids of the same age. Churches and cultural centers often offer language and culture classes as well. Becky's kids take Chinese at their local Buddhist temple, celebrate Chinese New Year at the Chinese Cultural Center, and her family also attends a lot of cultural celebrations at the Ethiopian Orthodox Church.

- **Host an exchange student.** Becky's family had an Ethiopian exchange student (who now lives in Norway) come to stay, and it was a wonderful way for them to learn some words in Amharic.

Becky's website, **kidworldcitizen.com**, is a great resource for adoptive families (or anyone interested in multiculturalism). Don't miss her article entitled: "14 Ways to Incorporate Birth Culture into Your Children's Lives".

Trilingual families

> *The more the merrier - three languages (or more) are possible.*
>
> Kendall King & Alison Mackey in *The Bilingual Edge*

Words from the wise

There are many situations in which having just two languages simply isn't enough for the family to communicate. This is the case when, for example, the family is already bilingual, uses the OPOL approach at home and has the community (and possibly school) language as a third one. Alternatively, the third language might be used by another caretaker or family member. Parents may well ask how many languages are too many, but experts say children will speak as many languages as they need to communicate with their environment. Therefore, as long as language acquisition is based on the need and desire for the child to use that language to communicate – instead of happening artificially, through means such as language classes, as we saw in Chapter 2 – parents don't need to worry about the number of languages.

However, what parents *do* need to pay attention to is that their children have sufficient opportunity to practice and have quality interaction in each of these languages regularly. From a linguistic point of view, the mind seems capable of learning several languages, but the challenge a family may run into is providing their children consistent exposure and meaningful interaction in all of the family languages within the time available.

The same basics apply to acquiring three or more languages as they do with two: a child needs to be exposed consistently to each language, and this exposure needs to be regular and long enough for him or her to learn to speak it. Since this is not always easy, or even possible, it is very normal that not all the child's languages are at the same level of fluency. However, experts stress the importance of making sure that at least one of the languages is developed at an age-appropriate level to ensure normal cognitive development. It's important for parents to remember that languages are never "done" and even the first (or "strongest", if you prefer) language needs continuous support.

View from the front lines

Many years ago, when I was doing research for my thesis, I stayed with a Finnish-Italian family that was living in French-speaking Switzerland, and came across trilingualism for the first time in my life. The lovely couple I was staying with had a five-year-old son,

Jonathan, who was one of the most inventive and creative kids I've ever met. What impressed me even more was how he spoke Finnish with his mom, Italian with his dad, and French with everybody else. There was a lot of support for French and Italian in his living environment, and he spoke those languages as a native. Even if his Finnish might not have been at a native-level in every aspect, it was still very fluent, thanks to the many trips they took to Finland.

I recently met the couple again when they were visiting Finland and asked them about Jonathan. They told me that their son, now 20, still spoke native-level French and Italian, had very functional Finnish, and in addition, had learned a few other languages at school. Keeping the three languages at this level had not always been a smooth ride, they told me, and over the years, the Finnish mother had needed to find many fun ways to keep her language alive and interesting to her son. It had paid off; Jonathan has become increasingly interested in his Finnish roots and had recently thanked his mom for not giving up on his Finnish, even if he would still have been bilingual without it.

Not everyone is, or has to be, as proficient in three languages as Jonathan to benefit from trilingualism. Many parents don't have as much support in their living environment for all of their languages, and most agree that finding the time for and exposure to all three (or more) is difficult, even when they all exist to a certain extent in the environment. Even in the best-case scenario, few are equally proficient in their multiple languages, as they are exposed to them in different ways and to different degrees.

Many of the ideas presented for bilinguals, including making a plan and choosing the language approach, also apply to raising children with more languages. Here are a few additional thoughts and suggestions from parents based on their experience of trilingualism:

- **An extra language is not always better**. It can be a good idea to introduce a third language to your child if it's natural and useful to them, but not just for the sake of being trilingual.

- **Children will not automatically become trilingual if their parents speak a third language between themselves**. They may pick up words and get used to the sounds of the language, but they don't learn to speak it unless people interact with them in that language, and they need it for communication.

- **Improve your own skills in the minority languages that are not your native languages**. If you speak the majority language, you can help your children in such activities as reading stories or playing games with them from time to time in one of their minority languages.

- **Support minority languages, but also the majority one**. Try to increase input for the minority languages, but don't forget the importance of a solid foundation in their strongest language, which will help them with the two others as well.

Single parents

I have many friends who are single parents, several of whom are also bringing up bilingual children. I have, on a few occasions, got a taste of their lives when Gilles has worked abroad for a few months, and this has made me very appreciative of the moms and dads in these one-parent families, and what they accomplish, even without bilingualism in the mix. I must admit that on the occasions when I've been the only parent running the show, making sure that my children have enough exposure to French hasn't always been my top priority, with everything else that's been going on.

Still, there are many single parents who successfully raise their children bilingually. If you are a single parent and a native or non-native speaker of a minority language, speaking that language with your children is very much like the mL@H situation. The minority language is your family language, and they learn the majority language outside your home. However, if you are the legal guardian of your child and you don't speak the minority language, and there is no (or infrequent) contact with the absent parent whose native language it is, you need to find ways for your child to meet other speakers. Many ideas that we will look at in Part 2 of this book will help, but here are a few to start:

- **Nannies and babysitters** are very useful in a one-parent family under any circumstances, so why not make sure they speak your minority-language? Alternatively, look for an immersion daycare or a bilingual school.

- **Connect** (for instance, on Facebook or on parenting forums) with other single parents who speak the minority language, and look for an arrangement to help each other out with babysitting and language learning. Network and connect with other parents raising children in the same language in your area, and ask them about the things they've found useful.

- **Work on improving your own language skills,** first by learning simple phrases that you can use with your child throughout the day, then by learning enough to read stories, however simple, in that language. In Part 2 of this book, we will look at other things you can do to reinforce the language with materials you can buy or find online.

- **Even a passive or limited knowledge of a language is valuable,** and can be built on later. Remember this if things get difficult.

Part 2 – Putting it into action

Up to this point, it has all been about theory, decisions on how to proceed, and what strategy to choose. Now it's time to look at how this plays out in everyday life. In this part of the book, my aim is to provide practical ideas for everyday situations and the different members of the family.

Chapter 7. ***From family strategy to personal strategy***

Let's go back to the language strategies for a little bit. By now, you have probably chosen a strategy for your family and made a commitment to stick to it based on the goals that you set earlier (knowing that both the goals and the strategy can be revised if need be). Your next question might concern what the concrete plan of action for you entails. This will likely depend on your role in the multilingual family and for this reason I have, with the help of tips and advice from other parents, put together some general ideas for each member of the multilingual family according to the language approach chosen and their role as the majority or the minority language speaker. There are some overlapping ideas, so to avoid repeating the same things, I would suggest, regardless of your strategy, that you read through it all.

Practical ideas for OPOL families

Ideas for the parent who speaks the non-community language

The French-Finnish school in our city is almost downtown, about 20 km (12 miles) from where we live, and accommodation prices close by were out of our reach when we enrolled Emma there. We only had one car, which I needed for my work at that time, and it wasn't possible for me to drive Emma to school. This meant that Gilles needed to catch two buses to take her there every morning, and yet another one to get to work; and do the same in reverse later in the afternoon. Many people couldn't believe that he would do this on a daily basis and wondered out loud if it was worth the trouble. Gilles, however, claimed that these moments alone with Emma were a fantastic opportunity to speak to her in French about all the things that were happening in her life, which was evolving mainly in Finnish.

Using the OPOL approach, your role as the primary source of the non-community language is essential for your child's language acquisition. Before you panic about this huge task in front of you, relax! **You basically just need to be yourself,** and act normally in your own (or your chosen non-native) language with your children. You are *not* their teacher (unless you choose to be, but we'll get to that later) and just knowing that should take some of the pressure off. Just be natural and make speaking your language a relaxed, ordinary thing for your children.

Now that you (hopefully) feel more relaxed, let's go back to what I just said about you needing to be yourself. It's true, but not the whole story. To be honest, it might sometimes be beneficial to enhance the "normal" you just a little bit. If you are not a talkative person, try to become one with your children! **Make a conscious decision to interact** (by speaking *and* listening) with your children as much as possible. With small babies who don't answer back, we can still talk about the things that we're doing – even if it's just about peeling potatoes for dinner. With older children, we all know as parents that there are numerous occasions during the day that could lead to great conversation and interaction, but we don't always seize them because we are tired, or have other things on our minds. Nobody's asking you to be superhuman, but try to look for, and take advantage of, opportunities to use your language in a natural context.

Look for one-on-one time with each child in order to benefit from a monolingual situation without the interference of the community language. You might not be able to relate to the bus example (public transportation is not as popular in many places as it is in Finland), but you can look for similar occasions to spend time together. Perhaps you have a hobby or an interest that you share? This provides an excellent opportunity to associate your language with fun and relaxation together. At times like these, children tend to talk the most, especially if we remember to ask many open-ended questions, and give them our full attention. The most important thing to respond to is what they tell us, not how they deliver it. Therefore, don't focus on correcting the mistakes they make, but instead rephrase what they said, and show them that you understood what they meant.

Jump at the chance to read as many bedtime stories as possible to your children. Yes, I know that you're tired after work and it would be so easy to have your spouse do it - maybe your child even requests that it be read by the other parent in the community language. Don't give up; every story counts as part of the language exposure of the day and stories are a great way to expand children's vocabularies. Talk about the stories, too, and ask questions, questions, questions.

Be consistent in using your language – even if your child replies in the community language! We will look at different strategies to deal with this later, but consistency on your part is key here.

Find support. By now you're probably wondering if you should read any further, as all this might sound like a lot of work and pressure placed on you. The good news is that you don't have to do it all on your own. Get connected with other speakers of your language and use their help to increase language exposure in your children's lives. Try these options to look for other native speakers of the language:

- **Contact your local embassy.** They might have a cultural section that organizes events to meet other people of your origin. In many French embassies, a Bastille day reception is organized for the nationals living in that specific country, and that provides a good opportunity to meet people. Find out what your embassy does.

- **Search Google and Facebook for expat or other international groups in your city**; chances are there are some speakers of your language there (check also **meetup.com** and **internations.org**).

- **Meet people at the Chamber of Commerce** or **Junior Chamber of Commerce,** if these types of organizations are interesting to you.

- **Network with your friends and colleagues. Word of mouth** is very effective. Put the word out there (in person, as well as on social media, and on bulletin boards at universities or community centers) that you're looking for families who speak your language, and someone will probably know someone who knows someone.

Help your children (if the situation permits) to create close relationships with grandparents, aunts, uncles and other relatives in your country of origin. I would suggest that you make as many visits as finances allow, and encourage your family members to come and visit you, too. Connect your children with your culture and help them feel part of it. As we will see later, this will be one of the best solutions to some issues that are bound to arise, including your child's occasional resistance to or difficulty with speaking your language. If you no longer have any family members or friends in your country of origin, it's still possible to visit and get the maximum benefits out of your trip. Read on for more about this.

Ensure that your children are never embarrassed about speaking your language. If you feel awkward about speaking your language in public, pause to think about what might be causing this, and, if possible, try to get over it. If it's because some people are rude and stare (and listen to other people's conversations) then it's up to you as a parent to show how to react. My advice would be to ignore it. If you lower your voice and seem embarrassed, your child will pick up on this and feel that there is something wrong with being linguistically different.

If, however, you don't want to speak your language in certain situations to avoid excluding other people you are with, try saying things to them in the majority language first and then repeating it to your child in your language. Personally, our family has never been in a situation where this would have been a problem once we'd explained our language strategy to the people in our group, and we have always made sure we've translated so that everyone knew what was going on.

Discuss your bilingual plan with your spouse regularly to make sure you are in agreement with the family goals. If your other half doesn't speak your language, encourage him or her to gain at least a receptive knowledge and help in any way you can. If this doesn't work, do your best to include your spouse in family situations by translating (or having your children translate) so that no one feels left out. If this is a conflict issue, try to work out a compromise everyone is happy with – for example, you could use a common language when everyone is together.

Remember that no one is, nor has to be, perfect – life isn't either! Set realistic goals for your children's bilingualism based on the time and effort you are able and willing to invest in it as a family. If it is a high priority for you, great, but make sure language development doesn't take priority over family harmony and healthy relationships. Avoid criticism at all costs and don't correct the errors your children make directly. Instead, just repeat naturally what they said using the correct form, and praise them for every step they make on their bilingual journey!

Last, but not least: make sure you find a good babysitter who speaks your language so that you can regularly take a well-deserved night out on the town with your spouse!

Ideas for the speaker of the community language

I love to speak and want to participate in every conversation, game, or event. As the speaker of the community (thus majority) language, I've noticed that I need to be careful not to dominate conversations, and to give sufficient time and space for my husband to interact with our children in his language. Sometimes this means removing myself from the picture for a few hours, or for an afternoon. Do I feel left out? Not at all: there's still plenty of time for the whole family to be together. Besides, there are times when a few hours of me-time is just what the doctor ordered!

Let me first ask you a question: do you think that your role in raising bilingual children is not important because your spouse is the one speaking the non-community language? If you answered yes, think again! **Your role in making it happen is far more important than you may think.** Your spouse is doing their best, but even in something as natural as speaking your language to your child (and even more so if they're speaking a non-native language), there can be moments of doubt, fear and frustration, and your encouragement and support are very much appreciated when this happens.

I'm sure you are aware of the numerous benefits of bilingualism. Still, you might have some concerns that prevent you from fully supporting your spouse. Let's briefly address these first, as for the whole family's sake it's important that both parents agree on the language strategy. Children are very attuned to their parents' feelings, and if they feel reproach from either towards speaking the non-community language, chances are they won't do so.

If you feel reluctant about family bilingualism, this might be because...

...you don't speak your spouse's language. One way to look at the situation could be as a great opportunity for you to learn. Even just a passive understanding of the language will do wonders for family communication and mealtimes when not everything has to be translated all the time. Don't get me wrong - it's a great exercise for your children - but it can become tedious on a daily basis, and you'll end up laughing at the fun stuff after everyone else. If you are expecting a baby, or have recently become a family, you have time to learn the language with your baby. However, if you have older children, and don't feel like having your spouse as your teacher, take a look at language classes or find a tutor through **The Mixxer** or **mylanguageexchange.com**.

There are also many good language learning apps for smart phones and tablets that you can use even if you only have a few minutes. Just google the device that you have and your language, for example: "android (or iphone) apps French". If you're still not convinced, and don't want to learn the language yourself, try not to feel excluded when you don't understand everything. If this is really difficult for you, to the point of interfering with family harmony, discuss your concerns with your spouse, and try to look for an alternative solution for mealtimes, and other occasions, when you could use a language that everyone understands.

...you're afraid that your parents or other family members will feel excluded from conversations that your spouse has with your children. How about talking it over with both your spouse and the family members in question? When the situation is explained to the extended family members, so that they understand the value it represents to their grandchildren (or nieces and nephews), many will not see a problem with this. If, however, you think that this would turn out to be a major source of conflict, perhaps a compromise can be reached. Some families have found it useful to use a common language in such situations, whereas in others, the parent in question might first explain to others what will then be told to the children in the other language.

...you feel that your spouse's language is of lesser importance globally, so its transmission is not all that important to your children. Without going back to the numerous benefits bilingualism (with any two or more languages) has for your children's development, it might be a good idea for you to stop and think about the importance to your children not globally, but within their own family, of learning the languages of both parents, regardless of what languages they are? What if the tables were turned and your language was the one with less global prestige; how important would it be for you to have your children learn your language?

None of these may be of concern to you, but if they are, the fact that you're reading this shows that you're willing to look for answers to any of the issues you may have in order to be able to give your support for what your spouse is doing. Once you're comfortable with that, here are a few ideas on how to do it:

Show interest and excitement over the progress your children are making in their minority language, even if you don't understand everything. Make sure they know that you approve of and encourage their bilingualism.

Give your spouse some alone time with your children for activities in the minority language. Let him or her read the bedtime story or involve your children in activities that are important in the culture that is part of the minority language. One parent offered me a great example: same-nationality dads got together with their children once in a while to cook and spend an afternoon surrounded by just the minority language.

Encourage warm relationships between your children and members of your spouse's family. Grandparents, aunts, uncles, and other relatives are an incredible asset to your children's development on many levels, and in particular, for their language skills. Spending time with the grandparents in a monolingual situation is a priceless activity to assist in their linguistic development, so it could be a great idea to let the children visit them without you, and also invite them for a visit. Even if there is friction between you and your in-laws (as might sometimes be the case), try to put this aside and think of your children's best interests.

Just because you don't speak the minority language with your children doesn't mean that you can't help them learn it! I don't underestimate the importance of my contribution to the French skills my children have today. Without having actually spoken the language to them (except recently), I have probably put close to an equal amount of effort into them learning French as my husband. You can actively help your children learn your spouse's language by connecting your family with other speakers of the language, organizing playdates, and looking for books and other materials – even traveling to a country where the minority language is spoken, without the native-speaking spouse. From now on, I shall refer to this country as the *minority language country*. You may also see it referred to as the *target country*. Our children and I have often spent several weeks in our minority language country, while their French dad has been working back in Finland. This has worked very well for our family.

Practical ideas for mL@H families

Ideas for the native speaker of the home language

Having a home language for the whole family can be very advantageous for transmitting your language to your children. You and your spouse might both be native speakers of the language and the community language is therefore left outside the home. In this situation, it is very easy for the family to create a home that is not only linguistically, but also culturally, like "back home". The only difference is that the external environment is not like that back home, and even with both parents speaking the home language, it will probably need to be reinforced against majority language influence. In rare cases the opposite is true, as with some of my students who come from immigrant families, and live in isolated minority language communities. Even if these students go to school in the majority language, many of them don't mingle enough with the native population to learn it except to a level of conversational fluency. Many of their friends outside their own community are also foreigners, and they learn broken Finnish from each other. If something like this is the case for your family and your children, it might be beneficial to verify that they get enough exposure, and associate with native-language speakers of the majority language as well.

In the other case scenario, where your spouse is a non-native speaker who is helping you to create a home where only (or mostly) your language is spoken, it can be important for you to give support in this. The children will realize, sometimes even quite early on, that one of the parents is not a native speaker and can even make mistakes. Here are a few ideas from parents on how the native-speaking parent can offer spousal support:

- **Avoid criticizing or pointing out the mistakes your spouse makes**, especially in front of the children. Give praise for the effort, even if your spouse is a fluent speaker and you think cheerleading is not necessary.

- **Explain the situation to your relatives** so that they do the same during visits.

- **Look for reading material and movies** that your spouse might enjoy in your language to develop vocabulary.

As for you, the native speaker, many of the ideas that were presented for the speaker of the non-community language with the OPOL approach still apply. Remember that you also need to be exposed to other native speakers, monolinguals if possible, of your native language. When we live abroad for a long time, our own language sometimes becomes sloppy or tainted with interference from the other languages we speak. In our family's case Gilles also needed to learn some "girl talk" that he had never needed growing up with two brothers. Since then, Emma and Sara have made sure that he knows the proper terms for different items of clothing and hair accessories.

Ideas for the non-native speaker of the home language

> Looking for Emma's balaclava in the dead of Finnish winter, I called Gilles and asked him if he had seen it. I knew the word "cagoule" in French, but not being a native speaker, mistakenly used the masculine gender form. Emma looked at me with round eyes and said "Mommy, why would you say le, it's la cagoule!" She was three-and-a-half years old, and I had a Master's degree in French! At the time, she was just genuinely surprised at someone making such a mistake but today, at age 12, she is merciless. Whenever I make a mistake, she corrects me, and adds: "And you're supposed to be a French teacher!" I just smile at this – but make sure that Gilles backs me up.

At some point, you might notice that your children speak the language better than you do. Don't let this bother you; instead, consider it a victory – what you're doing works! However, have your spouse support you and point out that it's not your native language (and that you're still doing very well), just in case your children make fun of any mistakes. Your own attitude will make a big difference here, too. If you don't get offended, but consider it helpful for learning (even thank them in a nice way), chances are they will want to help too instead of making fun. Some parents say they resort to their native language when they need to have all their authority with their children, and that would be one of the times I would use Finnish, too. However, for those who exclusively use the non-native language, a family policy where you can only criticize what is being said, not the way it's said, can be a useful one to implement before the children become teenagers.

Many parents also use terms of endearment in both languages, because, despite their good language skills in the home language, they feel like telling their children they love them and calling them cute names in their native language.

Last but not least - and this goes for both parents in an mL@H home - don't be upset if, despite all your efforts, your children speak the community language between themselves. This is a common phenomenon and one that parents have little control over. The best you can do is to reinforce the home language in ways we will look at in the next chapter.

All approaches – practical ideas for the extended family and friends

"I think we're lucky. My parents, my siblings, my grandmother, and one of my aunts keep inundating my children with books, CDs, magazines, games, etc. My sister also shared all the links to the websites her children enjoy. When we travel back home, they always try to help us organize interesting activities in which the children are immersed in the language."

A reply from a parent to "How can the extended family help?"

Even though you might not be in daily contact with these children (who may be your grandchildren, nephews, nieces, etc.), your role in their bilingualism can be important if you so wish. This is especially true if you're a native speaker of their non-community language.

Parents said that the most important thing they would ask of their extended family was for them to be supportive of the family's bilingual goals. This may not always be easy, especially for grandparents whose own children are speaking a foreign language (possibly not understood by the grandparents) with their grandchildren. They may feel excluded, and if they live in the same country with the family, they might question the importance of learning the other language. On the other hand, the grandparents in the country "left behind" may feel that they're just that: left behind. They might think that not enough effort is made for the children to get to know their language and culture. Here are a few Tried & Tested ideas for both sets of grandparents (but can also be used by other family members) based on what many parents said they would ask for if they had the nerve to do so.

Grandparents in the country of residence

- **Try to accept and support the fact that your grandchildren speak a language with one (or both) of their parents that you might not understand** or judge necessary. Think of it not as being against you, but for the benefit of the children.

- **Help the family with their bilingual goals** by complimenting the children on the fact that they speak two or more languages at such a young age. You might even ask them to teach you some words in their other language. Such endorsement will go a long way towards helping the children value speaking their non-community language.

- **Be proud of your grandchildren and the skills they have,** but please don't ask them to show off their language skills to your friends. As one parent put it: "they're not circus animals".

- **Encourage the parents when they're frustrated.** Remind them of the importance of having patience and that every child is different and shouldn't be compared with others.

- **Be interested and avoid criticism and negative comments**
about the other grandparents' way of doing things in their
culture. This is true for families living in the same country too,
but especially so in a multilingual and multicultural context.

Grandparents in the minority language country

Even if your grandchildren live far away, you can create an emotional
bond with them. Here are some Tried & Tested ways to do this:

- **Use different ways to stay in contact with them**: postcards,
letters, emails, phone calls or, better (and cheaper) yet: Skype. If
the children are old enough, see if it's possible to skype with
them from time to time without their parents, so that you can
talk to them directly. We've noticed that it's very difficult to
have the children talk in a natural way when the whole family is
speaking in front of the computer. In our case, the grandparents
sometimes skype with Emma after her school day before we, the
parents, get home. If your grandchildren are teenagers, create a
Facebook or a MySpace account for yourself – that's where the
teens are!

- **Try to accept as natural the fact that the children might not
speak your language as well** as that of the community they
live in. Be happy and congratulate their parents on their
accomplishment if the children are able to communicate with
you - and even if this is not the case, embrace the role you can
have in helping them learn their heritage language. This doesn't
mean that you need to teach them the language; just interact
with them naturally as you would with your monolingual
grandchildren. If you are willing and able to do so, ask the
parents if there are materials in your language (books,
magazines, etc.) that they need, or wish for you to send them
from time to time.

- **For birthdays and special occasions, think of gifts that are related to your language and culture.** For small children, it might be talking toys, DVDs, or CDs with children's songs. You could even buy a recordable story book and read the story on it in your language. For older children, comic books or subscriptions to magazines that are suitable for their age group and interests are great gifts that keep on giving throughout the year. If you're not sure about what to get, ask someone in your community who has children that are the same age.

- If finances and other circumstances allow, **visit the family in their country of residence,** and reciprocally, invite them to stay with you during their vacations (but don't be offended if they are unable to travel). Suggest that the parents take some time for themselves and leave the children with you for a few days or longer, depending on their age and situation. This will improve both your relationship with the children and their language skills.

Here are a few tips for when your grandchildren visit you:

- **Expect that they will understand you** when you speak to them naturally. Point and repeat like you would to any child, but don't speak to them as you would to a foreigner (unnaturally slowly or over-articulating). Even if they don't understand every word, they will figure out your meaning through your gestures, expressions and tone of voice.

- **Don't compare them with your other grandchildren** linguistically or otherwise. Look for progress, but not where they might be lacking compared to monolingual children.

- **Help your grandchildren integrate** by looking for other children their own age in the community for them to play with. Don't emphasize their differences. There is no need to keep telling everyone they meet that they live abroad and might not know this or that.

Your role is very important to your grandchildren in many ways, but especially linguistically. You are in a key position to help the family to reinforce their minority language, which is the topic of the next chapter.

Chapter 8.   *Reinforcing the minority language*

For as long as we can remember, Gilles and I have dreamed about having a house in Finland and another in France. We would divide our time between our two homes, spending our summers in Finland and winters in France. We haven't given up on that dream yet, even if financial obstacles, day jobs, and kids' schooling are in our way. In the meantime, though, we've needed to be creative to reinforce French, which continues to be our family's minority language – only for the time being, of course.

Words from the wise

All the experts tend to agree that if a family's goal is to have their children become active bilinguals, then it is usually necessary to reinforce the non-community language. The influence of the majority language is very strong and most bilinguals are, to various degrees, dominant in the language of their community. This dominance can easily change when the majority language changes when the family relocates to the minority language country. Due to the pull of the local community language, the minority language is vulnerable, whichever language strategy the family decides to use. This is all the more true if only one parent is responsible for input in the minority language, and this same parent is often away from home. If dominance in favor of the majority language becomes strong enough, the children may stop using their minority language altogether. To prevent this, experts suggest that parents support the minority language in different ways in order to make speaking it more interesting and attractive to their children.

View from the front lines

Some time ago, I attended an interesting talk on bilingualism. The speaker was very knowledgeable and talked about different things parents should consider when bringing up bilingual children. The one thing she didn't talk about, however, was the importance of reinforcing the minority language. After the lecture, she invited questions, and I asked her about this, referring to our own experience and how we felt that the community language easily became dominant unless steps were taken to reinforce the non-community one. The lecturer agreed, but before she had the time to comment on it, many parents wanted to jump in. One after another, they told the audience how in their case, their children had no problems with the minority language, and the community language was not even remotely dominant. Quoting their own words, their children were real "success stories" of bilingual upbringing. Nevertheless, as they talked on, one thing became very clear. Most of the parents making these claims were mothers with small children below four years of age who had stayed at home with the minority language-speaking parent and had only recently started kindergarten in the community language. It had been very easy to control their language environment until now. Many parents of older bilingual children, however, confirm the importance of reinforcing the minority language as children grow older and have more and more friends and activities in the majority language outside the home. Here are some ideas on how to do that.

Introduce other speakers of the non-community language into your child's life

Other native speakers or bilingual families in the community

Parents agree that it is very useful to meet other families who are using the same language for activities where the children can use the minority language in a natural context. This can definitely be easier in some places than in others, and many parents lament the fact that it's not always easy to find others in a similar situation, especially when you don't live in a big city. We will talk more about this in the next chapter and look at some tips on how to make it happen.

Babysitter

Look for recently-arrived expat families that have teenagers and ask them to babysit your children – in the minority language, of course. They will probably be very happy to earn some money of their own and your children will have a great opportunity for language immersion. If you don't know expat families, go back to Chapter 6 to find some useful websites to help you with this. You could also post ads at your country's embassy or a local cultural center in order to find such families. Another option is to look for students studying that language at university or other educational institutions. On a trip to the U.S. last year, we needed a babysitter for our children for one afternoon. Through a site called **sittercity.com** we were able to find a babysitter who spoke rather fluent French. More important than their own language skills, the babysitter should provide an opportunity (and a need) for the children to speak the language.

Au Pair

Having a native-speaking au pair live with the family can be a great way to increase the amount of minority language interaction in your children's daily life. This may sound like a more expensive option that it necessarily is (typically the main costs are room, board, and pocket money), but there are big differences around the world. In Europe, au pairs generally work for about five hours per day and get paid around 50-75 euros per week, depending on the country. However, in the U.S, they are usually the primary caregivers (working up to 45 hours per week) and earn about 200-250 dollars per week. The overall cost will also depend on whether you have to pay an agency fee, or for airline tickets and language classes, so it's best to start by checking what is valid for your country of residence. There are many organizations that specialize in finding au pairs. One such place is **aupairworld.net.** Click *Au Pair Programmes* on the home page, and look for your country.

When choosing an au pair, it's good to ask about motivations for going abroad. If the main reason is to learn the language of your country, it may be difficult to count on your au pair to speak your minority language at all times. If you take her personal goals into consideration and assist with them - allowing attendance at language classes, giving enough free time to practice your majority language outside the home, and perhaps with you when the children are in bed - chances are your au pair will also take your family's goals seriously. It's important to make sure that he or she understands that their role is not to teach their language to your children, but just speak it naturally with them, even if they don't understand everything in the beginning, or prefer to answer in the community language. If your arrangement includes chores around the house, you could encourage your children's involvement so that they can learn vocabulary in context in different situations.

There are also alternatives to having an au pair the official way:

- **Invite younger cousins, nieces, or nephews from the minority language country** to stay for a summer, or even longer with you.

- **Check with universities and cultural centers for students that are already in the country,** speak your language, and might be interested in exchanging babysitting in their native language for room and board.

- **Place an ad in a newspaper in the target country** (this is how I personally became an au pair in France, after seeing an ad posted by a French family in a Finnish newspaper).

When Emma was small, we got an au pair from France by accident. We had posted an ad on the notice board at the French cultural center looking for French-speaking babysitters, and were contacted by a young Frenchman looking for work in Helsinki. We got to know and trust him, and he continued to babysit for us in the evenings, even when he got a day job.

At one point, he had problems with his accommodation, and we made a deal that he could stay in our spare bedroom and in exchange, babysit Emma in the evenings as Gilles and I were both working late in those days. The arrangement lasted for about six months, until he found a girlfriend, and it was very beneficial for Emma's French.

Exchange Student

Just like au pairs, exchange students from the target country can be a great way to make the culture and the language more interesting to the children. Little children often like to imitate teenagers, and they can be great language models.

However, if the country they've come to is one they wish to learn the language of, it's not fair to ask them to speak their native language. This is especially true for the exchange students who come for the whole school year. Instead, try these:

- **Find out about shorter programs which focus more on the cultural experience** than language learning. This often varies seasonally, so check what's going on in your local area at different times of the year.
- **Look for a pen pal for your child from the minority language country** through sites like **epals.com** or **studentsoftheworld.info**. Maybe they can come for a visit one day.
- **Meet families who are hosting exchange students from your minority language country** and ask them to babysit your children from time to time. Even if the students are in your country to learn the community language, I know from personal experience that a few hours of speaking your native language and some pocket money don't hurt.

Find out about daycare or schooling options in the minority language

I can say, without a doubt, that our children's French skills have benefited greatly from attending a bilingual French-Finnish school. Roughly half of their classes are held in French by native French teachers, and the other half in the community language, Finnish. We are lucky, of course, to live in a place where such a possibility exists. Had our family language been something else, such as Italian, things would have been very different. An Italian I met a while ago lamented the fact that there was no organized day care or schooling for Italian-speaking children in Helsinki.

Studies have shown that the language spoken at school has a very strong influence on children's language use, and schooling in the minority language can for this reason be a great way to reinforce it. There are many different types of bilingual schools (or foreign language immersion programs) around the world, and your local embassy or cultural center will probably be able to inform you about the types of official programs that exist nearby in your language. Many of these programs and schools operate privately, which mean financial sacrifices to many who decide to enroll their children there. However, if such a possibility exists where you live, find out about available scholarships or tuition waivers before deciding against this option.

When we talk about our children's education, there are also other aspects to consider with regards to choosing a school. When faced with a decision about an establishment, ask yourself the following questions:

- **Would you choose this particular school if it didn't have the language aspect?** Would it still have the elements you consider to be the most important in your children's education?

- **Is the school's aim to help children transition to the community language**, or to actively promote bilingualism?

- **Are the teachers qualified** or are they teaching just because they are native speakers of the language? If they are not natives, are they proficient enough in the language?

- **What type of pressure would attending the school in question put on your family** in terms of expense, driving time, and possible extra tutoring?

In our case, being able to answer "Yes" to the first two questions helped us live with the fact that the school was far away and we would spend a lot of time taking the kids there and back. Based on our experience, I would suggest that you visit any school that you're considering (even sit through a few classes), and talk to other people whose children are already attending. Do keep in mind, however, when hearing about their experiences, that different families are looking for different things in a school, so what is positive for one may be negative for another.

Case in point: when Emma was small, we heard great things about a French-speaking daycare center. We decided to research the place and noticed very quickly that it wasn't a good fit for Emma. While the teachers spoke French as a native language, most of the other children were either beginners or spoke French at a much lower level than her, and we felt that she wasn't going to progress in this group. I would suggest that you find out whether the language program is meant for students learning a second language or for native speakers of that language, as the needs of these two groups are very different.

If no official schooling exists in your language, the expat network in your city might know about **Saturday schools** or something similar which are organized by same-nationality parents. If not, you could perhaps start one yourself with other parents. Saturday schools in different languages, and with different degrees of formality, take place around the world; in some, the parents take turns themselves to do the teaching, and in others they hire someone else to do it. Even so, it's good to remember that even if we parents feel that it is important to educate our children in their minority language, they might feel differently about going to school when their friends are having fun during the weekend. Explain to them the long-term benefits of doing this, but don't forget to throw in some short-term rewards too.

Homeschooling is another option that many multilingual families choose to make sure that their minority language is not crushed under the influence of the community language as their children start school. While this type of education is not yet readily accepted everywhere (for example, it's illegal in Germany and discredited in many other countries), it is considered a viable option in many other places. In the U.S., for example, many view homeschooling a much more efficient way to learn than in classrooms. There are homeschooling groups, which do activities and field trips together, and provide social interaction in the community language. This way a child who is home-schooled in the minority language at home also has sufficient access to the majority language. For more information on the topic, check **homeschoolingonashoestring.com**. I would also highly recommend visiting the Multilingual Living Website (**multilingualliving.com**), and ordering the digital back issues of Multilingual Living Magazine. In addition to the magazine being filled with all things interesting related to multilingualism, the founder of the magazine, Corey Heller, is an expert on bilingual homeschooling.

Some parents enroll their children at a school in the community language and homeschool their children part-time in their own language to teach their children to read and write. Others prefer to have a tutor help their children with this. Whichever choice the family makes, biliteracy is a great way for the language to evolve from basic conversational fluency to a higher competence in both languages.

Encourage biliteracy

There will be a time when you no longer read stories or books to your children, but they will read them on their own. When this time comes, not only will they choose what they read, but in this case, also the language they read in. Unless your children are actively encouraged (and in most cases, instructed) to learn to read in their minority language, they probably won't. This would be a shame, as reading in a language is very valuable to its development: it helps build vocabulary, increases grammatical knowledge and gives access to the culture the language is linked to. Through reading, your children's knowledge of the language matures, and this development transfers to speaking skills in that language as well. The best part is, if we parents play our cards right (and we'll talk more about that in Chapter 10), it can be a lot of fun for our children, too.

According to experts and parents, children most often learn to read in the language they go to school in. The Internet is full of stories of two-year-olds who have learned to read in two or more languages by themselves. Meanwhile, back in the world where the rest of us live, most children learn to read when they're between four and seven years of age - even if research does seem to indicate that the thinking-related benefits that bilinguals have can make them predisposed to learn to read earlier than their monolingual peers. There are no hard and fast rules on when would be the best, except when your child is ready and expresses an interest. Until then, there are other easy ways to prepare your children to read and write, which means exposing them to varied spoken language through speaking (and listening), playing different games with them, and reading stories to them. Lively dinner conversation is important on many levels and not in the least to lay down a foundation for literacy in the form of strong verbal skills.

Some children develop reading skills in all their languages simultaneously; others (the majority) one after the other. It would seem to be easier to learn to read in the most dominant language first, especially if the second language is a lot weaker. Reading in a language that the child is fluent in is gratifying and opens the gateway to literacy. This can then be built on and the acquired skills transferred to learning to read in the other language. However, if your child is fluent in both languages and is schooled in the community language, it could be useful to introduce literacy in the minority language first before school starts. Children receive a lot of support in reading in the school language and therefore usually progress faster than in the minority language. Learning to read in the home language first could help to avoid possible competition with the school language, and comparisons between the pace of acquisition of literacy in one language and the other. Parents have found this to be especially true when the two alphabets are very different. Of course, your child might have his or her own ideas about this, but we'll cross that bridge in Chapter 10.

Being able to read is one thing, but actually doing so is another. Are you creating an environment where reading is valued and where your children have interesting written material readily available? Next, let's take a look at where such materials can be found.

Look for electronics and non-electronics in the minority language

First write to the overseas publisher with your order. The publisher will send back the prices. You then send back an international bank draft for the correct amount in foreign currency, and the publisher sends the material. This can take several months to accomplish.

Jane Merrill about buying materials from abroad in *Bringing up baby bilingual*, 1984.

I don't know about you, but personally, I'm very happy to be raising our children bilingually today, rather than 25 years ago. So many materials and resources are available to us, and thanks to the Internet, we can access them very quickly and from anywhere in the world. Here are some Tried & Tested ideas about materials that can be useful to a bilingual family.

Books

We've already touched upon the importance of biliteracy, which not only helps our children to develop a deeper fluency in both languages, but also to gain access to the cultures in question. Trips to countries where the minority language is widely spoken, as beneficial as they may be, are not always possible as often as we'd like. This is where books from the minority language country come to the rescue and instantly make the children part of that community, which is sometimes oceans away. As we have seen, immersing children in the language through meeting other speakers, preferably children, is very important. However, to have access to the language in all its richness, with vocabulary and nuances, there is nothing that can replace immersion in children's literature. Books present children with a different vocabulary than what their parents use, and fill in the gaps that they might have in their language skills due to not living in a country where that language is widely spoken. Reading books to children in both languages (with an emphasis on the minority language) is one of the fundamentals of a bilingual upbringing, and one that can make all the difference in terms of their language development.

Where to find books in a foreign language depends largely on where you live and what the language in question is. The following ideas should get you started:

- **Check your local library.** If you are lucky, they may have books in your language or they can order them from another library. If you can convince the librarian that there are many parents who would be interested in borrowing books in a certain language, they might even acquire some new ones for their collection. Also, embassy cultural centers sometimes have their own private libraries, so it's worth checking with them, too.

- **Exchange books** with other families who speak the same language in the community. You could maybe even set up a "library system", where everyone writes a list of the books they have, and you can ask to borrow the ones you like. Alternatively, organizing a book swap with families means you can get new books in exchange for old ones that the children are no longer interested in.

- **Look for a family in your minority language country who has the same language selection,** and kids about the same age as yours, and suggest sending each other books. The books in your community language are easy and relatively cheap for you to find, and you know what your own children like to read. The same is probably true for the other family in their community language. An attempt to get such an exchange going between bilingual families is the page **facebook.com/ BilingualBookswap**

There are also sites for book swapping that work internationally, such as **bookmooch.com**. On Bookmooch, you earn points by providing someone with a book they want and can then use these points to get books from other people. The service is free and you only pay for the postage. The great thing about this is that from the English language main site, you can access seven international sites – in German, French, Spanish, Portuguese, Japanese, Italian and Swedish. I've even found many Finnish books by locating fellow Finn bookmoochers on the site. You can also install a browser toolbar called "the Moochbar", that you can use to first search for books at bookseller Amazon, and then see if they're available for trade on Bookmooch.

- **Find books for sale.** Simply typing "books" and the language you're looking for (e.g "books french") into an Internet search engine will give you lots of results. However, first check locally with expats or other families who speak your language and have older children; chances are they still have some children's books and might be willing to sell them to you cheaply.

Our family knows something about book hunting, as we've tried for years to find French books at the rate that Emma reads them. This is what we've found:

- **Children's book clubs that send a new book every month (even abroad) sound good, but we ended up paying a lot for books she didn't read.** Not all the books were interesting or suitable for her, but returning them from another country ended up being too much of a hassle for us.

- **Online secondhand bookstores have become trusted friends.** Some deliver abroad, but we've usually ordered books from **livrokaz.com** (that also has a book swap system) before traveling to France, and had them delivered to the French grandparents' address. This way, we've just needed to remember to reserve one suitcase to bring all the books home.

- **amazon.com has also been a good source of books.** You can get new ones, but they also sell secondhand books and deliver them to our door in Finland. Whenever I find interesting items on Amazon, I also check if they're on **bookdepository.co.uk**, which offers free worldwide delivery.

- **The launch of Amazon Kindle in French was a real breakthrough for our family:** Emma received two of her favorite books in French with just a few clicks (and no postage). Kindle has recently been launched in Spanish as well.

When the minority language- speaking parent is absent, **recordable storybooks** are an interesting option. For the moment, many of these are targeted at English speakers (sold by Hallmark and Toys "R" Us in English-speaking markets, and accessible to others through Amazon), but the recording can be made in any language. Hallmark also carries something called **conversation books,** where you can record your conversations with your children about the book. You can, of course, use any language you wish, even if the prompt text is in English.

Magazines

Your children will learn a lot about the cultural references of their counterparts in your minority language country from magazines.

These are especially useful to children who can already read. When appropriately chosen for the right age level, magazines contain articles that are likely to interest your children and motivate them to read in the minority language.

There are magazines to suit all tastes and interests, such as sports, princesses, horses, crafts, science, comics, and so on. For teenagers, a teen magazine can be a great way to get into that country's popular culture, which at that age is important. A subscription to a magazine that arrives by mail every month can make both the country and its language interesting, and is a great gift for birthdays or other occasions.

Many magazines can be ordered abroad directly from the publisher or through sites that specialize in selling subscriptions from multiple publishers to people living outside the country. One such site we've used for French magazines is **unipresse.com,** which makes it very practical to compare the offers of different publishers. Still, subscriptions abroad remain relatively expensive, and we've found it cheaper to buy back issues of the magazines and have them delivered to the French grandparents' address. I used to do this a lot when the children were smaller and didn't care whether it arrived by mail or was the latest issue or not. I would keep them in a drawer and take out a new one every month, or even more often, depending on how long the previous one held their interest.

Just like books, magazines can be exchanged and borrowed from other families, too.

TV/DVDs

There is a lot of controversy surrounding the watching of TV and DVDs, and the expert consensus seems to be that for children under two, there is no need for it, and in larger doses it might even be harmful to their development. For older children, it can be a tool to complement language learning, but by itself as a passive medium, it can't really be counted on to do much more than that.

The main purpose of TV or DVDs is to show that the non-community language exists and has prestige in its own country in the same way that the community language does in the country the family lives in. To see local TV shows or DVDs from the other home country is a great way for your children to learn the cultural references of others their age living there. This makes things easier when visiting relatives and making new friends during their stay. In addition to this, you could also try to look for programs or films that your children already know and like in their majority language; it can be motivating for them to watch those again in the minority language.

TV - Practical aspects

How can you watch another country's television programs, other than paying large sums for satellite or cable? The websites **beelinetv.com** and **wwitv.com** offer free online TV channels from around the world. However, they only work intermittently and the quality is not always very good. We use **captvty.fr,** which allows us to watch French television shows online for free two weeks after they air in France. We usually save them on a USB memory stick and watch them on our family television set rather than on the computer. Try googling "catch up TV" and the name of your country of origin to see if something similar exists in your language (for German, **www.save.tv,** an online video recorder for German TV, was recommended to me).

Many TV stations, especially the commercial ones, don't allow the viewing of their programs from abroad. This is also true of the website **hulu.com** in the United States. Hulu makes it possible to watch hundreds of programs for free via the Internet, which would of course be most interesting for American families living abroad, but viewing is blocked outside of the country. Some parents have found a (perfectly legal) way around this by using a VPN (Virtual Private Network), which lets you connect to a computer located in the target country, making it appear as though you're actually there. To get this, try **vpnUK.net** or google free VPN services.

I recently also came across something called the **Slingbox**. It's not a free option, but is still interesting if you have someone in the minority language country who is willing to let you connect to their TV system. The Slingbox is a small box (hence the name), which you buy along with a computer router (unless it's included in your Internet services), that connects to the other country's TV and your existing broadband connection. This way, you can view satellite, cable, digital and analogue television over the Internet from anywhere in the world. You can also watch it live and use a virtual remote control as if you were physically there, or connect to a DVR to record programs.

The one big inconvenience is that while doing this you are literally taking over the TV in the other country. The best case scenario for this would be to have more than one TV source at the transmitting end, and have only one of them connected to the Slingbox.

DVDs - Practical aspects

The great thing about DVDs is that with portable devices, you can pretty much take them anywhere. We have had many pleasant road trips with two happy kids in the back seat watching DVDs in French. We have never bought a single DVD in our majority language, but instead, whenever we're in France, we stock up on age-appropriate local entertainment. These include films, but also more educational DVDs like the *C'est pas sorcier* series, which is of more interest to our tween than the children's films. Little by little, we have also built a "dvdthèque" of all the classic French films that Gilles wants the kids to see as they grow up.

When buying DVDs from abroad, remember to check that the region code matches the DVD player you have at home. While you can find advice and instructions online on how to hack into DVD players and make them zone-free, another less messy solution is to buy a region-free DVD player and then you never have to worry about this. Many cheap no-name brand DVD players don't have the region code set on them and will play DVDs from any country. Alternatively, you can also play DVDs on your computer.

Where to get them

If you didn't buy DVDs when you were on vacation in your minority language country, and don't have family or friends you can ask to send some over, check the DVDs you can buy at home. Sometimes they come with several language tracks, and might include your language if the countries are geographically close. A lot have options for common international languages like English, French or Spanish.

Many parents recommend **amazon.com** as a good place to find DVDs (google "amazon foreign language movies section", and choose "by original language"), but not all items can be delivered internationally. Should this be the case for something you wish to buy and you don't have anyone whose address you can use in the minority language country, there are online services that can create an address for you in the US, the EU, or some other location, which then forward your purchases to your home address. One such site is **bongous.com**, which can package multiple items into one shipment in order to lower the price. Another site for American addresses is **myus.com**, but these are just suggestions; shop around to find what's best for you. To take full advantage of this consolidation process, you could join forces with other parents in your community who are in the same situation and make a group order.

In the spirit of collaborative consumption, try your luck in finding and exchanging DVDs in your language with other families or on sites such as the **swapadvd.com.** When using a VPN (like the one for TV), it's also possible to buy and watch **movies on demand.** If you are also speaking French, you could try **fnac.com,** but there are other sites that offer this service in other languages. You can also share movies or music files (which are not copyright protected) with family living in the minority language country through **gigatribe.com**, which is a peer-to-peer private file sharing network. You download their software, connect with relatives and download each other's selected files. I have only recently discovered this, but it has quickly become my new favorite.

Both TV and DVDs are passive media, which mainly increase your children's interest rather than skill level in their minority language, but there are some ways their linguistic skills can benefit from them. In addition to watching the DVDs together and talking about them with your children, you can buy toy characters from TV shows or films. Both our kids loved to watch *Lilo & Stitch* in French. On a business trip once, I found small plastic figurines with the main characters, and Sara played with them for hours, going over the dialogue she had picked up from the movie. The online Disney Store sells figure sets of the main characters from many of their movies. Incidentally, the Disney movies are often dubbed into many languages, so it might be easier to find one of these films in your minority language.

Music

Music and rhyme are fantastic tools for learning. Music improves listening skills and helps fix things in the mind – I was reminded of this just recently when I heard the melody of a TV commercial from the 80's and noticed that I still knew the words by heart! For over 40 years, children have been taught alphabet and numbers using advertising-like jingles on *Sesame Street*. Now, on the Internet, **earwormslearning.com** uses this strategy to create products that combine music and language learning. They are currently working on products specifically targeted to children.

Songs teach vocabulary, rhythm, and cadence, especially if you sing together with your child instead of just listening. Look for a book with traditional songs in your language (preferably one that includes a CD), and check **mamalisa.com** for songs and rhymes from around the globe in original languages. YouTube is also a great source of music from all over the world (and you can find lyrics to almost any song on the Internet). We use an audio editor program called **Audacity** to save music from YouTube on our computer.

Radio

Radio plays a big role in our daily routine of making our home more French. Listening to programs from France helps us parents keep up with the language and what's happening in the country, but having it in the background also familiarizes our children with French music and contributes to the French atmosphere at home. In the car, we listen to children's radio in French through smart phone applications, and connect the smart phone to the car's audio system with an FM transmitter.

The World Radio Network (**wrn.org**) offers news and information from broadcasters worldwide, while another great website that can be used to access international radio wherever you are is **mikesradioworld.com**. There are over 5000 radio channels from all over the globe to choose from – chances are you'll find your local one there, too.

Tunein.com has a great selection of children's radio stations from around the world. Click on "children" as a music genre and scroll down until you find the stations in your language.

Board games and other traditional games in the minority language

Games not only provide a fun way to use the language together with the family, but prepare your children culturally for visits to your minority language country. The same games are played by monolingual children in that country, and make for a natural and easy transition and integration. In addition to traditional board games from the minority language country, I recommend looking for an international edition of Monopoly linked to that country, city or region.

Computer games

Most children are probably going to play computer games anyway, so why not get them some in their minority language? Many parents have reported finding good ones on sites like **ebay.com** in addition to Amazon, or local bookstores and supermarkets in their minority language countries. Depending on the language, you will probably find some that teach the language, but they are often meant for monolinguals and might be too basic for bilingual children. Instead, look for games in or from the country: computer games are pretty self-explanatory, so your children will probably figure it out, even if the language is more complicated.

Internet

You can find almost anything online, and there are some great sites for different languages. The problem is mainly that there are so many, and you need to figure out which ones are good. Here are a few general ideas, but please check our website for more language-specific suggestions.

- **Videos**. We know YouTube is great, but there is so much out there that you could spend days just looking for and reviewing the material. A few websites can help with this. The site **bookbox.com** features animated books with subtitles in over thirty languages; **kideos.com** is another one, but it caters mainly to English speakers. For teens and adults, **viki.com/channels** offers episodes of TV shows and movies from different countries through YouTube - the idea is good and it might be worth following how the site evolves, even if there is not a lot of content yet.

- **Online books**. One good site for this is **childrenslibrary.org**, which is a free online library with around 4,500 digitized children's books (both classics and contemporary) in 55 languages. Another one, **childrensbooksforever.com**, offers lovely old-fashioned stories and illustrations by Hans Wilhelm in PDF format in a dozen languages. Read them online or save them for offline use. For those who, like me, love *The Little Prince*, you can find online versions of the book in over 40 languages at **petit-prince.at**.

- **Websites for children.** Word-of-mouth is the best way to find the good ones in your language - ask other families, check our website and please share the ones you've found useful with us. There are real jewels to be found, such as **labbe.de** for German, which contains hundreds of children's songs with lyrics and melody, games, stories, and creative ideas - all for free.

Smartphones and tablets

The rate at which technology progresses is amazing. When Emma was born, we considered ourselves modern because we had huge cell phones that could hardly fit in our pockets. The webcam image on the computer (which ran through the phone line) was blurry and strange, and we couldn't show her French video cassettes in Finland as the PAL/SECAM video standard made cassettes purchased in one country black and white when played in the another. We could not have imagined the things we can do today with our phones in addition to calling people – like watching videos in color, or skyping!

Here are a few ways in which you can use your phones and other computing devices to promote your children's bilingualism and interest in their minority language.

- **Audiobooks.** Since Emma was starting to read, we have bought French storybook / CD combos (like the series *Mes premiers j'aime lire*), which the kids can read and listen to at the same time. Many times, our children have wanted to take just the CD along in the car and listen to the stories. With new technology comes new possibilities, and the Amazon-owned **audible.com** offers audiobooks for mobile devices such as the iPhone, Android, or mp3 players. You can either subscribe to it or buy audiobooks as a non-member. The subscription costs a certain amount per month and gives you credits that you can buy audio material with (for example, at the iTunes music store or the Amazon Appstore for Android). International websites exist for France, Germany and the UK, but even the American site sells content for children and adults in several languages, although mainly in French, German, and English for the moment. For speakers of other languages, Google is your friend here. Type in your minority language, along with the phrase "audio books and podcasts for children", and cyberspace will most likely deliver.

For other audio (and video) content, visiting the iTunes store of your minority language country offers interesting possibilities if you have access to a postal address and a local bank card in that country. Create an account that is separate from any account you might have in your country of residence, and you should have no problems purchasing audio and video files for any device that will play digital files.

- **Educational games.** There are lots and lots of interesting games for smartphones and tablets which contribute to language learning, and many contain test version you can get for free and a full version that costs a little to install. The other day I downloaded a free test version of a game called Smart Speller for Sara in both French and Finnish. The French one was very good and I ended up paying two euros for the full version; the Finnish version, however, was uninstalled a few seconds after we started playing. It was clearly a translation of the English version that no native speaker had checked, so it's advisable to try them out first yourself. In addition to different games, you can find flash cards, stories, apps that teach you how to spell and read - you name it! I would suggest you do a search in your minority language on the net for the best language learning apps and games (and then please let us know so we can share it on our website).

- **Videos.** The app **Children TV**, by **CyberWalkAbout.com** finds child-appropriate videos on You Tube and rates them by language, fun, and age. There are over 800 cartoons in 10 languages for children between 2 and 8+, and it is available for android and iPad.

All of the above can be great supplements to your child's language learning, but they will not replace the one crucial thing: interaction with other speakers of the language. The motivation to learn, and the need to use the language doesn't come from playing computer games, but from wanting to communicate with others, as we shall see in the next chapter.

Chapter 9.   *Mingling with the natives*

A few years back, I heard a story about pelicans in California. Their great numbers had been a real tourist attraction in Monterey Bay for many years, but the situation had changed unexpectedly and the pelicans had started to die. Experts, biologists, you name it, flew in to study the problem, which was soon linked to the extinction of the local tuna fishing trade. It was found that the pelicans had been leading life a little too easy for their own good, following the fishing boats and feeding on their catch. Now that the fishermen and their boats were gone, the birds were confused and hungry - they no longer knew how to hunt for food! Not having had the need to actually find and catch their food had meant they gradually lost the ability to do so.

A solution was found in the form of pelicans that did know how to hunt. They imported hundreds of them to Monterey Bay from Florida, where they had been hunting for food in the normal pelican way. They quickly adjusted and started doing the same in California. Surrounded by these "natives at fishing", and motivated to follow their example, the local pelicans also began feeding and the crisis was averted after just a few months.

Finding "pelicans" in the community

Words from the wise

Sometimes, speaking the minority language is like catching fish in this story. If the children don't have a need to use the language, it is very probable that they won't and the skill is then slowly lost. Experts tell us that children require first and foremost a need and a motivation to use the language, and suggest that surrounding bilingual children with natives, preferably other children, often presents the best opportunity for this. Wanting to play with and be understood by other children seems to be one of the best motivators for a child to use his or her second language. The minority language becomes a natural means of communication, and any self-consciousness about possible errors or gaps is quickly forgotten when the children concentrate on playing and just getting the message across.

View from the front lines:

So, how do you go about it? The easiest and most efficient way to accomplish this is by taking the children from their usual surroundings and into the natural environment of the second language. A trip to your minority language home country, or to another country where that language is spoken, is definitely a fantastic way to solve many issues related to the acquisition of that language. However, the country in question may be far away and a trip not possible for many reasons. Here we can learn from the pelican story. Just as the local birds reacquired skills from the foreign birds flown in, our children can learn from the children in our community who speak the minority language. Try these ideas:

Look for (or organize) playgroups with other speakers of your minority language - and cross your fingers that the children will play together using that language. This happening is the best-case scenario, if all the other children also speak the majority language. Parental experience seems to show that the older the children, the less likely they are to use their minority language the moment they figure out that using the majority language is an option. We may care about them speaking our language, but all they will care about is using whatever is the easiest and most efficient way to get the message across.

Activities organized by a native-speaking parent are therefore a good way to get your children to participate, and why not invite some "pelicans" to join the playgroups? Perhaps you could look for recently-arrived expat families - there might be Facebook groups, the local embassy might have lists or cultural activities where you can meet them, and word-of-mouth is also a very good way to find out about new arrivals. They might be very happy to meet locals, and your children could make new friends that are (at least for the time being) monolingual speakers of their non-community language.

Become a host family for couchsurfers. Sign up with **couchsurfing.org** to host travelers that speak your language. This can be an option even if you can't accommodate the travelers in your home. Many are happy just to get to see the city through a local's eyes.

Take advantage of modern technology, which offers many ways to connect children with other speakers of their minority language. If you have family in your target country that has access to a computer, then Skype is a must. For children to actually see and talk with grandparents, uncles and aunts on a regular basis is a great way to keep in touch with both the family and the language. This creates emotional ties with the language and makes things easier when traveling to meet the family.

Similarly, you can stay in touch with other families that you may have met during travels in the minority language country, in order to extend and create friendships with other people and children who speak the same language. If none of this applies to you, how about looking for other families through language exchange sites like **The Mixxer** or **mylanguageexchange.com**? Alternatively, you could post about finding Skype partner families who speak your language on forum websites such as **multilingualliving.com**.

The girls' grandmother in France recently got a computer for Christmas. The first thing we did was to install Skype on it with instructions about how to contact different family members. As Emma comes home from school in the afternoon and turns on her computer and Skype, grandma often calls her and they talk - just like they might if she lived next door, and not 2000 km away! They can have a private conversation, which can be as short or as long as they wish, since it's free. As it turns out, grandma is often privy to a lot more information than we parents are!

Going native – traveling to your minority language country

Words from the wise

Experts agree that traveling to a country where your minority language is the community language has many advantages, the first one being that the children will probably have a newfound respect and appreciation for the language, as they see that it is not only spoken by mom or dad, but by a whole nation on a daily basis. There is an actual need and motivation to use the language to interact with locals, and this will yield great results, especially if a little planning is done to make sure that some interaction actually happens. Just breathing the air in another country will not have any effect on your children's language skills, whereas interaction with locals, preferably children, will.

View from the front lines:

Before traveling to the target country most parents are excited, but maybe also concerned about how to make the most of the trip, especially if the country is far away and can't be visited that often (I speak from experience when I say that the trip can be a financial sacrifice, and for this reason I've added some moneysaving tips at the end of this chapter). Those who are not boarding with family or friends need to think about places to stay and how to provide opportunities for the children to practice their language skills. The ones with family have different concerns, maybe about living with the in-laws for several weeks. Both might worry about the children and how they will manage with the language and be accepted by other children, friends, or even family members.

Among the first things to decide is the length of the trip. Any length is better than none, but seeing as it takes about a week for children to completely adjust to a new language environment, anything less than that might not allow them to fully benefit from the experience. Between two and four weeks seems to be a good length for a stay (the longer the better, really), but with careful planning even shorter trips can be useful in giving the child's language skills a boost and providing the motivation to use them. For financial reasons or to avoid the crowds, many families travel during the off-season. This is understandable, and based on the feedback from parents, you will find many Tried & Tested ideas for interaction with other children outside school vacations.

Traveling on your own

Accommodation

If you're not staying with family or friends on your trip abroad, the next thing to decide is the form of your accommodation. As tourists, your children will hear the language everywhere, which is great, but it's even better if your family can mingle with the locals. Hotels might not be the best option for this, but if you want to stay at one, look for these when booking:

- **A mini club or a kids' program**. These kinds of clubs are a good place for children to play with others, but unfortunately only expensive resort-type hotels usually have them.

- **A hotel close to a park where children play.** You can check this with the tourism office.

- **Family reviews** on a site like **Tripadvisor.com** to see if many families visit the hotel, and what suggestions they have for children.

However, hotels are not the only places at which you can stay. Here are a few other suggestions that you might want to consider, especially if you are willing to get away from the big cities:

- **Hostels.** As **hostelbookers.com** states: "Hostels are no longer just a stomping ground for students and backpackers – clean and comfortable rooms now attract a diverse range of visitors looking for cheap accommodation." Many hostels offer private family rooms and a kitchen for all the guests. **Hostels.com** is another site on which you can look for a suitable hostel.

- **Bed and breakfasts in private homes**. These places tend to be run by locals and can be a great gateway to meeting people and integrating into the life of the town. As local residents and business owners in the local tourism industry, your hosts can be very resourceful about things that are bound to interest you, or at the very least, they will know who to ask in town about activities for children. Try **bedandbreakfast.com, bed-breakfast-world.com,** or contact the local tourism agency at your destination.

- **Rent a house.** Renting a house can get you very close to the locals, and if you are in the countryside, it can be much easier to approach people than in cities. You can do ordinary things just like the locals, such as grocery shopping, and chatting with storefront cashiers and the mailman. You are part of the community, so why not ask the family next door over for coffee and cake so that their children can meet yours? To find out about house rentals, read **Frommer's online guide to vacation rentals.** You might also want to contact the local tourism office where you are going, or look at the following websites: **homeaway.com** or the quite interesting **airbnb.com** and **housetrip.com,** which rent out private apartments and houses to suit every budget and taste.

- **Home Exchange.** Friends of ours have done this several times (through **homeexchange.com,** but we've also heard good things about **homebase-hols.com**) and they talk highly of the experience. In addition to allowing for a better cultural experience, it has the obvious advantage of being free (except for a small agency fee). Of course, swapping houses with complete strangers can be a bit daunting, but getting to know each other on Skype before the planned vacation can make things easier, and provide linguistic benefits, too. If this works well, I would even take things one step further and ask the family if they know other families with children with whom you can organize playdates while you are living in their house. This can be a great way to integrate into the community.

- **Camping sites or holiday parks.** Less glamorous than a nice hotel, if that is an issue for you, but unbeatable when it comes to kids finding other kids to play with. Ask the tourism office for suggestions and search the internet for forums where you can double-check the information to make sure you find a nice one. If you're not the camping type, don't worry: neither was I. However, I can assure you that I changed my mind about that the minute the kids from the next trailer came to ask our children to play with them. Campsites are often jovial places where people easily get to know each other, and at many sites, teenagers or adults organize campsite activities for children. A lot of sites also have cabins or lodges if you don't feel like either renting a trailer or an RV, or sleeping in a tent (which, let's admit, can be somewhat awkward with suitcases).

- **House-sitting.** If you're willing to assume some responsibilities, like taking care of pets, mail and similar during your trip, your family could live rent-free by becoming house-sitters. Sites like **mindmyhouse.com** and **trustedhousesitters.com** can help out with this.

- **Couchsurfing.** Do you have an image of backpackers in their twenties sleeping on strangers' couches in your head when you hear this word? I did, but my information clearly needed some updating. The backpacking generation of the eighties and nineties has children now and many want to continue traveling in the same way with their families. If you've got some adventurous spirit, look up some locals at your destination (who, ideally, have similarly-aged children) and ask to stay with them for a few days - it could be a great way to interact with locals and experience their culture. Enthusiasts claim that sites like **couchsurfing.org, tripping.com, bewelcome.org,** and **hospitalityclub.org** are attracting more and more families. Even if you don't want to stay at someone's home, you can contact families to meet them for coffee or ask them to show you their city.

Before making your choice, I would suggest you read family reviews about the accommodation you're considering on travel pages such as **tripadvisor.com** - chances are you will get a lot of information from just reading other people's reviews. Alternatively, you can post a question on the forum about your destination, explaining your situation and asking for advice based on that. The local tourist office is also a good place to consult before you make a choice. Whichever way you decide to go, make sure you book early, have travel insurance, and check that you all have valid passports.

Finding local activities for children when traveling on your own

There are times when being a tourist is a great thing, but this is one time when you want to blend in as much as possible with the locals. This doesn't mean that you need to skip all the tourist attractions, but it's good to plan ways for the children to meet other locals, and play with others of similar age. From them your children will learn the local "play" language and children's nonverbal behavior, which they won't pick up if they're only around adults.

In addition to the idea of contacting families and setting up playdates through organizations such as **couchsurfing.org**, you can look for an expat network in the area and ask them for advice about activities and places where your children could meet other children. Ask for tips and advice from locals on the forums of neighborhood parenting websites. You could also visit the local tourism office website or send them an email to ask for advice on your situation.

Travel communities such as **tripadvisor.com** are not only helpful when choosing accommodation, but are also great for ideas regarding what to do with the children in a particular city or smaller towns.

Depending on when and for how long you're staying, and what your children enjoy doing, here are a few ideas you might consider:

Going to school in the target country

Before you think that I'm crazy to suggest this, just hear me out: vacations don't always take place at the same time in different countries and, particularly if you're traveling during the off-season, it might be that the local children are all at school during the day. Many schools welcome children who live abroad but speak the language to spend a few days, or even a few weeks as guests. This can be a good way for your children to see what school life in the target country is like, and hopefully meet new friends. Perhaps you can find some expats online before you travel who could tell you whom to contact in the local school their children attend.

To prepare for the experience, your child (or even the whole family) can write a letter to the class and send postcards or something similar from your country of residence. This will not only prepare your child but the whole class for their initial meeting. Integration is also much easier for a familiar child that the class already knows. After a successful stay, your child can continue writing letters or even skyping with their new school friends.

Our daughters have successfully attended a local village school in France for the last two weeks of the school year. The exam season was over, and most days consisted of trips to the swimming pool, excursions, and preparing an end-of-school-year performance for parents. To tell the truth, our children were a bit reluctant at first, but they ended up really enjoying the experience, and made many new friends in the village. This made all the difference during our stay; trips to the pool and the library were so much more fun when there were friends that could be invited along.

I realize that this might not be as easy in big cities as in a small village, and if your children struggle with the language and are not enthusiastic about speaking it, this is probably not the option to start with.

Practicing with the locals

Many parents have told me they found enrolling their children in local swimming lessons to be an effective way to meet other children. The same idea can be applied to other types of lessons, such as horse riding, martial arts, or whatever is interesting to your children and available in their age (and price) range.

If your children have a social hobby at home (a sport or playing an instrument), why not ask the local clubs and organizations if they can participate as guests during your stay. Not only can it be motivating for the children to experience their hobby in the minority language - something they're already familiar with and can grasp the concepts of easily - but it can lead to playdates and friendships with local children. Last summer, Emma had a great experience with a French soccer team who welcomed her to practice and even participate in a tournament with them.

Summer camp

-   **Day camps.** Local libraries and community centers are great sources of information on what the local children are up to. They usually know (or can at least advise you where to ask) about day camps and workshops for children during school vacations. In France, for example, municipalities organize outdoor childcare (centres aérés), which corresponds to a day camp, during school vacations.

- **Overnight camps**. A great possibility for your children to mix with other children is for them to attend a camp for a few days where they can be immersed in their minority language. A good site to find all kinds of camps around the world is **kidscamps.com**. Again, the expat network, local parenting websites, the tourism office or local schools should be able to help out with this. There can also be camps that specialize in an activity your child practices or likes, so check those clubs and organizations, too.

Other

Get your children a temporary library card at the local library if their policy allows. We've noticed that libraries are always full of other children. On several occasions, I've successfully approached them, explained our situation, and asked if they could show Emma some books they like.

Visit the Global Greeter network's website (globalgreeternetwork.info), which brings together local volunteers who give free tours of cities. If you're in luck and your target city is on the list, take advantage of this great opportunity to get an insider's tips on the community.

Motivate the children to use the language by giving them a small allowance that they can use for small purchases – in the minority language, of course.

Always bring a few extra toys when visiting playgrounds, parks or beaches so that your children can invite others to play with them.

Staying with family members

Many of the ideas just listed can also work for those who have family to stay with, especially if there are not many other children in your family. Staying with grandparents or other family members offers the advantage of "living in the language" throughout the whole stay, and children have a real motivation to communicate with people who are important to them. In addition, parents might also benefit from some, or all, of the following Tried &Tested ideas.

Ideas for staying with the in-laws in the minority language country

We all know a whole book could be devoted to this subject, with or without discussing multiculturalism and multilingualism. Even if we love and appreciate our in-laws and everything they do for our children, when we are together for weeks, things are bound to get tense from time to time. Many of the following ideas may seem obvious (and good for you if they do), but a little reminder sometimes helps.

Whatever you do or say, keep in mind your children's relationship with their grandparents. Don't criticize the in-laws or their different ways of doing things. Instead, show your children in any way you can that you appreciate their grandparents and their cultural heritage (which, incidentally, is that of your kids, too). Yes, there may be tensions, but as adults we can at least try to set those aside for some days, or even weeks. If this is not possible, would it be better to have your children visit them alone, or with your spouse, and you stay at home?

Believe in your kids' ability to understand their grandparents. Some parents hover around their children at all times and translate everything their grandparents say to them, even when it's clearly not necessary. This might hinder the relationship between your children and their grandparents and conveys to the children that you don't believe they can get by in that language. If your children don't have to try to speak the language, they won't. Expect therefore that your children will understand and be understood, and give them some time with their grandparents to get to know each other (not always a given when living in different countries) and - sorry if this is tough - without you. Just look at the advantages: how often do you get the chance for some quality time alone with your spouse?

Time to loosen up. So they might have *croissants* and *pains au chocolat* for breakfast in France, and you'd rather they had something healthier. I can relate to you, but consider it an investment in their cultural heritage. A few weeks is not going to destroy their health (as it is, most French people are quite healthy), and it will add to many pleasant moments experienced in the minority language and culture. The same thing goes for the whole "grandparents and sweets" issue. You may limit the sugar intake at home, but if the grandparents don't take the hint after you ask them nicely, just take a deep sigh and look away. You'll get your children back on track at home, and they'll have many tasty memories to associate with the language and culture.

Knowing that I'm repeating myself, let me say it once more: **give the children time alone with their grandparents** (or uncles, aunts and other important people in their lives who are native speakers of their minority language). Some time is great, but more time is usually even better. Our children spend four weeks or more alone with their grandparents every summer and this has not always been easy for many reasons. Apart from the financial aspects and the criticisms we've received from other people, we have missed them and worried about them for many a summer – even if they've been in extremely capable hands. Each time, however, they've come back happy, suntanned and with loads and loads of stories in excellent French about everything they've done with Papy, Mamie, Tonton and Tatie, and we've congratulated ourselves for having listened to our guts instead of the critics.

Children traveling by themselves

For many families, a trip to their minority language country may be difficult for many reasons. Cost is one issue, but the other problem is that there just aren't that many vacation days in a year. Some families arrange for a sabbatical to really benefit from immersion in the family's second culture, but some look for ways to have their children travel, even if they can't go themselves.

If you have family that your child can visit in your minority language country, many airlines offer a UM (unaccompanied minor) service for children aged from 5 up to 12 (or in some cases older), who travel without an accompanying adult. From the moment the airline takes charge of the child at the airport, they are responsible for the well-being of the young traveler until the moment they release the child to an identified guardian at the other end of the journey. Airlines have different rules regarding the UM service, which may or may not be free, and can't usually be booked online.

Even if your child is traveling to a country that only requires a photo ID as a travel document (such as within the EU), get a passport for them and find out if either of the countries in question requires a letter of consent (also called "travel clearance"), and if this needs to be done at the relevant embassy or notarized. We learned this the hard way: Emma once missed her flight back home from France because she was traveling with a photo ID but without a letter of consent. This hadn't caused any problems arriving in the country, but France has a policy which doesn't allow sending French children abroad with merely a photo ID, even though the document stated that she lived in Finland and was, in fact, returning home. We had not been aware of this, and spent a stressful day at the French Embassy trying to obtain a paper which allowed Emma to travel out of France, although she didn't live there in the first place. This is not to put you off this option, but just to let you know it's good to check with your embassy what the requirements are. The same may also apply if the child is traveling with someone other than the legal guardians (like grandparents).

If sending your child to visit family as a UM is not an option, there are countless organizations that specialize in trips abroad for children, whether it be immersion camps or study trips for a few weeks or an exchange student program for a full school year. It is, of course, very important to check the organization in question and the way they ensure the safety of the children in their charge, and talk with other parents who have gone through the same experience. I personally spent three weeks in England as a 13-year old, and a year in the USA as a 17-year-old, and count them among the best experiences in my life. Without that, I might not be writing a book in English today.

After the trip

Be patient if your children's improved vocabulary or enhanced language skills are not obvious during the trip. Their brains need time to process it all, and many parents report that their children's new skills appear about two weeks after they return. This is also when their new motivation to speak the language is at its highest, so take advantage of this. Talk about the experience, write to family and new friends in the minority language country, and make good use of Skype. If you had your video camera with you, watch the film and spend time going through photos and talking about them. We've often spent many evenings together with the girls after a trip posting photos or making photo books on sites like **shutterfly.com**. We've written captions for the family to read – naturally, in the minority language.

Money-saving tips for traveling

I've often heard people say that bilingualism costs money and is therefore only for those who are well-off. My first instinct is to say that this is not true. There are many things that cost nothing: for example, you can talk to your child and do the everyday things you do anyway, but just do them in the minority language instead. As we've seen in previous chapters, there are also ways to get materials relatively cheaply, find them for free on the internet or make them yourself.

Yet traveling to the minority language country, the one thing that seems to make the biggest difference, does cost money. Not many of us have the financial means to design our lives the way we want to, and most of the time there is a trade-off of some kind involved in our choices. Being a very normal middle-income family, the trade-off for us has been to live in a relatively small house, and to have only one car. The situation became more difficult a few years ago when Gilles was suddenly laid off from his job, and our family's financial situation took a serious hit that lasted for almost a year. Going to France twice a year, as we had done until then, no longer seemed possible on top of trying to make ends meet. Still, our family travel being such a priority for me, I was determined to find a way to do it. Here are a few things that helped in our case:

- **Making a grocery budget**. Based on the money we had available, I budgeted a certain amount for food. I envied my friend in the U.S who had access to coupons (if you do, check out **fabulesslyfrugal.com**), but scouting for discounts helped me to plan meals that were healthy, made with fresh ingredients, but also very inexpensive. It was nothing fancy, but with careful planning we still ate well, and leftovers made a great lunch for me at work the next day. I took out the weekly budget in cash (with plastic it's so much easier to spend more), and everything that was not spent at the end of the week was saved towards our trip to France.

- **Finding a few private students** that I helped with French a few hours per week. I did this by posting ads at universities and libraries.

- **Having my bank automatically deposit a small amount of my paycheck into a savings account each month.** The amount was small enough to go unnoticed, but added up to at least one plane ticket a year.

- **Canceling magazine and newspaper subscriptions** (except the French ones for our children!). We could just as easily read the news online. I did the same thing for my gym membership, which was costing me too much for something I didn't use that regularly. We also changed telephone companies and electricity provider to new ones who were willing to give us better deals to have us as customers.

- **Watching movies on TV instead of going to the cinema** and having occasional fancy meals at home instead of going to a restaurant.

- **Selling things that I really wasn't using** (or children's clothes that were too small) on eBay and at flea markets.

The following summer, the whole family was able to travel to France, and during the spring break in February, we sent Emma as a UM, as we couldn't afford to travel as a family. I realize that the situation would have been different had our minority language country been further away, and I don't want to be insensitive to anyone in a difficult situation. Neither am I saying that you need to give up your lifestyle entirely to travel to your minority language country. It is up to each family to decide how much time and money is justified to achieve their family's bilingual goals. I merely want to share with you what worked for us in our situation. A habit that has stayed with me ever since is to put all two-euro coins I get as change in a tennis ball can. It takes me a long time to fill the can, but I know that once it's full, the four of us can travel to France.

When you're ready to start booking, here are some ideas on how to save on travel costs:

- **Check the right sources.** Thorn Tree travel forum on **lonelyplanet.com** and reviews on **tripadvisor.com** are examples of places where travel information is not created and paid for by a company, but comes from real people who've been there, done that, and sometimes quite literally bought the t-shirt. Take advantage of it before you pay.

- **Travel during the low season**, if possible. When you're visiting family or for linguistic purposes, the weather doesn't matter that much and travel prices are usually lower during these periods. If you do choose to travel during the high season, make sure you book early.

- **Join an airline rewards program.** By using the same airline or partner airlines, you can earn points (or miles) each time you travel, but many airlines also have affiliate programs with the following services that help you collect even more points when you present your frequent flyer number at the time of booking or check-in:
    - hotels and hotel chains
    - car rental companies
    - telephone operators
    - banks
    - online retailers

Many airlines also issue their own credit cards that help you get points from credit purchases and offer cheap companion fares. Visit the airlines' websites to find out the specifics for your market.

Different airlines have different policies for when their points expire and free tickets need to be booked well in advance. Even if the ticket is free, airport taxes still need to be paid. If you have points on several reward programs, you might want to check out **points.com** where you can trade, exchange or buy points.

- **Look for deals online.** There are simple search engines that help you find the best deals for plane tickets or hotel rooms by going through all the major sites for you, such as **kayak.com** and **travelocity.com**. If you find a good fare, check if the same is available on the airline's website, as you may get frequent flyer miles when booking through them directly. For those living in the US, **bing.com/travel** has a handy tool called "price predictor", which tells you whether it's best to buy a ticket now for your destination, or if the price is likely to drop in the near future.

- **"Name your own price"** on **priceline.com** lets you bid for airline tickets to a specific location and dates with one or two stopovers. You name your price, which according to Internet sources can be about 40% less than the official price, and your bid is either accepted or not. If it's accepted, you won't get the details until you've paid. Once you accept, your credit card is charged immediately, and there will be no refunds. Before you use this option, make sure you study how it works by visiting a site such as **biddingfortravel.com.**

- **Promotional codes and coupons** for airlines and travel agents can be found online. One interesting address for this is **moneyning.com**, but you can also try eBay and Craigslist.

- **Discount airlines** won't always show up in the regular search engines, but might save you money - or not. The thing about discount airlines is that they have a lot of hidden costs and often charge for things like checking in luggage, in-flight service and even seat reservations. Many of these airlines also fly out of and into smaller airports, which at times can be a long and expensive trip away from the city you wish to visit. They rarely, if ever, offer a frequent flyer program.

  Despite this, our family has saved a lot of money by using low-cost carriers within Europe. One important thing to know about these types of flights is that they're meant for point-to-point travel. There is no connecting flight system, even if the carrier lets you buy a connecting ticket on their website. Your luggage will need to be picked up and checked in again between flights, and should something happen, like the first flight is delayed and you miss the connection, the two tickets are considered to be two separate transport contracts, and the airline is not responsible. We have occasionally taken the risk when we've come across very cheap fares, but we haven't booked the next flight until the following day to try to be on the safe side. You can find more information and a search engine specifically for low-cost airlines at **flylowcostairlines.org**. Another useful site for finding budget airlines in you market (which allows you to find fares and book directly on their website) is **wikitravel.org/en/ discount_airlines** .

- **Save by flying mid-week, and in and out of the same airport**. You should do the same for car rentals: you end up paying a large drop-off fee if you return the car somewhere other than where you picked it up. Make sure you pay for your flights with a credit card. Credit card companies refund customers for services they didn't receive, and this is important as airlines have, from time to time, gone bankrupt without much advance notice.

- **Last, but not least: be careful with your money when traveling**. First, shop around for the best exchange rates for your currency. Second, instead of carrying a lot of cash or traveler's cheques, look into currency cards. You load money onto your card by phone or internet, and if your card is lost or stolen, your money is protected, just like with travelers cheques. Read more at **cashpassport.com,** or ask your bank if your country of residence is not on the list.

Several families I've talked with have not just one, but several minority language countries to visit. The choice of where and when will be affected by many factors, but check currency fluctuations to find out which one has the most favorable exchange rate at the moment.

Disclaimer: While I hope that the information I have presented here is useful to you, they are just ideas that I have used myself or people have told me about. I do not represent any commercial travel interests and I cannot accept responsibility for any of these suggestions or the consequences of any actions taken on the basis of this information. Do your own research on the things that interest you before taking out your credit card.

Chapter 10: *Tried & Tested – situations from the everyday lives of multilingual families*

In this chapter, we will look at some solutions that families have found to situations that are very common in multilingual families.

Situation 1. "My child doesn't want to learn to read in the minority language."

Emma learned to read in Finnish first. One day she just read what was written on the cereal box, and after that, there was no stopping her. She read everything and everywhere – but only in Finnish. There was really no need for her to learn to do it in French, which would have required more effort (something she wasn't a fan of to begin with) than mastering the very logical letter-to-sound correspondence in Finnish. Our attempts to help her to read in French only irritated her, so we decided to back off. However, that didn't mean giving up, but instead, going about it in a different way. Knowing how much Emma enjoyed jokes, I bought a book filled with them in French. One night, I casually read one of the jokes to Gilles out loud. This did the trick, and the book, left lying on the living room table, quickly vanished. It was too interesting for her to resist, and she picked it up out of her own free will.

We already know that biliteracy is important for many reasons, but our children might not be as enthusiastic about it as we are. While some parents find that bilingual children are naturally curious about the way both languages are written, many others would love to have a bag of tricks to motivate their children to read in their minority language. It never seems to work when we try too hard, so the key is to be less obvious and work our way around our children's resistance. I shared above what worked with Emma, but with Sara the situation is very different, and new tactics have been necessary.

Try these to make literacy fun for beginners:

- **Play alphabet games** such as "I spy with my little eye, something beginning with C..." You can play another alphabet game in the car where everyone is trying to find as many words that start with a certain letter as possible. Also, think alphabet soup and cutters for Play-Doh – or even better– real cookie dough, to introduce the alphabet.

- **Write words on windows** with window paints.

- **Organize word bingos and word searches** (with small prizes). You can find generators online that allow you to use your own words (in any language) for this. Two of these sites are **discoveryeducation.com/free-puzzlemaker** and **print-bingo.com.**

- **Use magnetic letters** on the fridge and write a word of the day for the children to decipher.

- **Look for board games** that help children learn to read in your minority language. Sara really enjoyed "Mon Atelier Lecture" in French. Scrabble is another one that can be found in many languages.

- **Label objects at home with sticky notes,** for example "chair", "table", "the door."

- **Have a mail-box inside the house.** Leave daily messages for your children; it's incredible how motivated they can be to read them.

- **Make your own place mats** with puns, riddles, jokes or activities. During a trip to the US, I noticed that many restaurants gave our kids place mats to color and write on while they waited for their meal. You can easily do the same at home with a pen and A3-size paper (just google "printable place mats for children" to get inspired). Don't forget color and pictures to make it look fun.

- **Play hangman,** the traditional game in which one player thinks of a word and the others try to guess what it is by suggesting letters.

Be savvy with these tips when your children can read to some extent (but just choose not to):

- **Continue to read to your child in the minority language.** There seems to be a consensus among reading experts that 30 minutes per day is when the magic starts to happen. Make your reading interactive and pause occasionally so that your child can read a predictable word that you're pointing at.

- **Find out what kinds of books your child really enjoys.** When reading such a book to your child and you get to an exciting part - where your child can hardly contain their excitement over what is going to happen next - suddenly remember something you absolutely have to do right away, and leave the room for a few minutes. If the need to find out what happens next is big enough, your child might pick up the book.

- **Write "secret messages" to your children.** Write fun notes in your minority language to put inside their school books. If you have the time and energy, organize a scavenger hunt and write clues in the minority language. Make it a party and invite other children who speak the language, too.

- **Write a riddle, a joke or a short story on A3-size paper and post it on the bathroom wall.** They can't escape it, and that's one place where they can decipher it in their own time.

- **Cook your child's favorite food,** but only if you get help finding the items on the shopping list or reading out the recipe in your minority language.

- **Switch TV and computer settings to your minority language,** then the language must be used to operate any home electronics.

- **Look for written material on topics that your children are interested in.** If they are excited about things to do on an upcoming trip, find brochures in the minority language. Do the same thing for their favorite sports team or bands. Ask relatives in the minority language country to send fun post cards, letters and comics. Encourage your child to write a reply.

- **Start a family blog, and write posts together with your children.** Ask family members in the minority language country to comment on the posts. You can use sites like **blogger.com** or **wordpress.com** to create a blog for free.

- **Organize a book club with other children in the same situation.** This creates positive peer pressure. Make sure you choose interesting books for their age level and offer a delicious snack afterwards.

- **Help them write emails to their future selves.** Emails that your children write on **futureme.org** will be delivered back to them on the specified date days, weeks or years later. This might just be fun enough for them to try it out – and make them aware of, and motivated by, the progress they're making.

To come back to the story about Emma, she did learn to read in French, but continued to prefer Finnish. When she asked to read her first Harry Potter, we weren't successful in motivating her to do so in French. After she had read the book, however, we looked for the movie dubbed into French. After this, it was she who asked to read the following books in French.

As for bilingual books (also called dual-language books), I feel the jury's still out on these. While many parents believe that it helps to see both the majority and the minority language side by side, my personal experience is that once the children have read the story in their dominant language, they have little interest in reading the same story in the minority language, which is, at this stage, more difficult for them. Even so, they like to hear the stories over and over in both languages. In our family, bilingual books have worked the best when we parents have taken turns to read the same story in our respective native languages.

Situation 2. "My child may have problems in speech development."

Even today, many people still believe that bilingual children are more prone to having speech problems than their monolingual peers. For this reason, many parents pay closer attention to how their bilingual children speak, and some, expecting problems, find each anomaly in their child's speech to be a sign of trouble. In the process, some forget that these are often the kinds of mistakes that monolingual children also make. As one parent pointed out, if you live outside your native country, you might not be exposed to monolingual children who speak only your language, and know the kinds of mistakes that they make. In addition to this, children develop different skills in different ways.

This is not to say that bilingual children don't have speech problems: they do, and in the same proportion as monolingual children. The difficulty lies in trying to distinguish communication differences, possibly due to the presence of two languages, from actual disorders. As a parent, you know your children best, so if you're worried, here are a few steps you can take:

- **Check the general milestones for speech development,** but remember that they're only guidelines.

- **Visit a pediatrician to check your child's normal development and hearing.** Remember, however, that pediatricians are not necessarily experts in speech development or bilingualism.

- **Look for the *Bilingual Communication Assessment Resource* (**by Larry J. Mattes and Cristina Saldaña-Illingworth) at your library or university. The book gives guidance to parents and teachers to help them examine their children's use of both languages in natural situations rather than in a test setting.

- **Consult a specialist if there is any doubt.** In an ideal situation, the speech therapist would be fluent in both (or all) your family languages. At the minimum, he or she should understand bilingualism and give advice other than dropping one of the languages. Unfortunately, people around the globe still report receiving this recommendation today, even if experts agree that this is rarely a good solution.

- **Look for professionals online, if you can't find suitable help where you live.** You can find resources and a directory of multilingual speech / language pathologists at **thespeechstop.com.** These might be able to assist you or at least help you determine whether you should be worried and what the next step should be. Another interesting option is the Canadian company **TinyEye (tinyeye.com)** that offers e-speech therapy sessions to people around the world. The winner of the 2011 Ingenious Award from ITAC, this company currently offers treatment in English, French, Spanish and Dutch, and with its European franchise, is planning to add many more languages to this list in the near future.

Situation 3. "My child refuses to speak the minority language!"

Younger children

> The same thing happened with both our daughters when they started to attend a Finnish kindergarten at the age of four. After speaking French exclusively with their dad until then, they suddenly asked him to speak to them in Finnish when there were other children around. Instead of doing so, we talked with the kindergarten staff and enlisted their help to put in a good word for our family's bilingualism. They were happy to help, and the other children were fascinated by the phenomenon, which was presented to them in a very favorable light. They even asked the girls to teach them some French words. In Sara's case, that was all that was needed, but Emma clearly struggled with French after days spent speaking only Finnish. "Daddy, let's pretend we're Finnish speakers", she suggested coyly when Gilles picked her up from the kindergarten. He didn't react to this, but instead just diverted her attention to something interesting – in French.

It's very natural that when your children grow older and start to do things outside the home, the community language can very quickly become dominant because they are using it so much. When this happens, your children may reject their minority language to a certain extent. Often, this can be fixed by increasing exposure, but even more importantly, by providing them with a need to use it, as we saw in Chapter 8.

How should you react when your children speak to you in the "wrong" language? You might feel frustrated, or even upset with your children when in fact, you should start by thinking about what has caused the situation. I want to insist that your children are not lazy, or rejecting you as parents, if they don't speak your language. They are simply lacking the need and motivation to use the language.

So the solution requires increasing their motivation. There are many different ways that parents use to deal with the situation when their children use the majority language with them. Here are a few ideas that you can choose from:

- **Pretend not to understand**. This may be a bit artificial as a strategy if your children hear you speaking the majority language with other people. One mother told me she explained it this way to her son: "I only understand that language when adults speak it to me."

- **Take a long time to do things when they make requests in the majority language**. Immediately attend to whatever is asked in your language.

- **Act surprised**, and ask: "Why are you using daddy's / mommy's language?"

- **Make the children repeat everything twice** when using the majority language, but they only have to say things once in the minority language.

- **Arrange meetings with other bilingual children**. They will get positive peer pressure when they see children of the same age who do speak a minority language with their parents.

- **Praise them whenever they use their minority language** rather than forcing them to use it.

- **Rephrase in your language** what they just said, and ask them questions as if to confirm that you understood: "You mean..., right? You want to..., don't you?

- **Move on in your language** without paying attention to the fact that your children used the other language.

Most parents agree with the experts in that the best strategies are those that don't interrupt communication, but help change the language as subtly as possible.

Teenagers

> *When you are a teenager, "No" is actually a complete sentence.*
> Author unknown

I may not be a parent to a teenager yet (although I feel we're really getting close with our 12-year-old), but I meet them every day at work in my classrooms and see up close what they go through. Identity issues and fitting in with their peers seem to be the most important things at this point in their lives. So it's not surprising if they feel reluctant to speak their minority language, at least in public. It makes them different from those around them, and that's exactly what most teenagers try to avoid. On the other hand, they might also be afraid of not living up to people's expectations as a "native" speaker of their minority language, and refrain from using the language for this reason.

It's understandable that, facing teenagers who generally speak very little, parents don't make the effort to get them to speak in the minority language on the occasions when they *do* communicate. Pushing them to use the minority language might cut the conversation short, and no parent wants that. The best course of action would seem to be to continue speaking the language ourselves (it is, after all, *our* language and we're entitled to speak it), and try to create a link between things your teenagers find fun, interesting or useful, and your minority culture and language. Here are some ideas for doing this:

- **Look for material in your language about things they're interested in,** such as a subscription to a magazine. Look for ways to put them in touch with peers who share the same interest in the minority language country. One way could be through specific websites related to the interest in question.

- **Introduce them to the popular culture of your minority language country.** Find out from friends or relatives (or through websites or Facebook groups) what teenagers in that country rave about. What websites do they visit? Who are the pop idols or sports stars from that country, and what are the latest movies that teenagers watch? As a teenager, I was a big fan of a Swedish boy band, which did wonders for my Swedish as I listened to their songs over and over again and looked for anything that was written about them.

- **Look for babysitting jobs for your teenagers in families that speak your language**. Such families probably want to increase language exposure for their children, and that suits your purposes very well, too! If you have younger children, you could enlist their help (for a reward of some kind) in reading bedtime stories in the minority language.

- **Show their friends that your language and culture are cool**. Seriously, if *they* think so, you've won half the battle. Throw a fun party for a cultural event and invite their friends over.

- **Look for recently-arrived expat families with teenagers and get to know them.** Facebook expat groups and embassy contacts are two ways to do this. Offer to take their teenager along with yours to an interesting outing (shopping or movies are usually good options) where they can get to know each other in a fun and relaxed environment.

- **Send your teenagers over to the minority language country** to visit friends and relatives, for a summer job, a summer camp, or even as an exchange student to attend a local school for a semester or two. They could also travel with one of the many organizations that specialize in sending young people abroad. One example of such a community is Youth For Understanding at **yfu.org**. Alternatively, travel there together without their other siblings for some quality one-on-one time.

- **When looking for communication with your teenagers, remember:** adolescents have different biological rhythms than adults. They tend to be most relaxed and apt to open up late at night. I've heard of parents who take a nap and get up around midnight to take advantage of this window of opportunity to discuss things with their teenagers in more depth than they can during the day. A midnight snack together can give you a lot of insight into their lives and make them more open to speak your language when there's no one else around. Another good place for conversations with your teenager is the car. There are no distractions and no one's looking directly at them. I've heard that this works even better if it's late (and dark) in the evening. Remember, however, to listen and not interrupt or prompt for an answer. They might need time to gather their thoughts.

- **Don't forget humor**. Look for jokes, comedy movies or TV shows in your language. As humorist Victor Borge said: "Laughter is the shortest distance between two people." Surely this applies to teenagers, too?

Situation 4. "My child mixes languages."

Most Swedish-speaking Finns mix their two languages together. The monolingual Finns often sneer at this, thinking that their bilingual peers aren't really proficient in either of their languages. As a matter of fact they are, and the mixing (often referred to in this sense as *code-switching*) is proof of this. When speaking with other bilinguals, they can take elements from one of their languages and insert them into the other while respecting the grammatical rules of both languages. This is done at times to emphasize something, or just because the word in one language conveys the meaning better. Many bilinguals use mixing as a social tool with other bilinguals simply because they can, but are quite able to stick to just one language when speaking with a monolingual person.

For smaller children, mixing doesn't usually mean that they are not able to separate their languages, but is instead just an efficient communication strategy. It is very normal that children don't have the same vocabularies in both languages, and if they can think of a word faster in one of their languages, then they will use it. Experts say that mixing is a normal phase in language development, and is usually temporary.

A few things you can do:

- **Ensure that your children have enough exposure to the non-community language in an unmixed form.** This might mean having to monitor your own language use and mixing.

- Use ideas from the earlier chapters to reinforce your children's minority language and increase their vocabularies. Read, read and read.

- Avoid correcting or punishing the children for mixing languages. Instead, find a way to repeat the word they said in the other language in a natural way, to teach it to them in case it's missing from their vocabulary in that language.

Situation 5. "I'm worried: what is my child's cultural identity?"

> *Children who are brought up to be bilingual have a sense of where they come from and feel proud of their heritage. These children sometimes describe themselves as being a bridge between two cultures.*
>
> Naomi Steiner MD, Susan L. Hayes and Steven Parker M.D in *7 steps to raising a bilingual child*

People who live in close contact with two cultures can learn to function naturally in both. I admire my husband who, after 18 years in Finland, operates brilliantly as a bridge between the two cultures and is for this, among other things, a very valuable asset to his company. On joint projects between France and Finland, he is the mediator who smooths things out between workers of the two nationalities, sometimes by making sure there is coffee that suits the Finnish palate, sometimes by teaching the Finns that yes, it really is necessary for them to shake hands and say "bonjour" to their French co-workers each morning. These are little things, but have made a real difference to their international projects.

Gilles has learned to understand the two cultures by picking up clues while living in both countries. Our bilingual children, however, have only ever lived in Finland, and there are cultural things that we needed to teach them deliberately. The fact that they are very fluent in the language sometimes makes their small cultural blunders seem like impolite behavior. Both girls have had a difficult time with the French custom of *la bise* (kiss on the cheek when meeting), which has surprised and confused their French family members. Similarly, they have been frowned upon for using the informal form "tu" for you, instead of the more polite "vous" form. The French people that our children meet in Finland seem to have grown accustomed to the Finnish informality; even their teachers at the French school go by their first names instead of *Madame* or *Monsieur*, which would be expected in France.

I know you know what I'm about to say: time spent in the minority culture country is, once again, the best medicine. While there, children can observe others, preferably their peers, and feel confident in duplicating the same behavior. Still, there are things we can do in our country of residence as well. Besides spending time with, and exposing your children to, others who share your cultural and linguistic background, here are a few ideas:

- **Celebrate your traditions**. Make a big deal of it, and try to make the celebrations as authentic as possible. I know it's not always easy, as traditions tend to blend. For example, we spend Christmas the Finnish way on Christmas Eve, and the French way on Christmas day.

- **Watch movies**. Our girls have picked up a lot of cultural clues from French movies. It really works.

- **Read books that are relevant to the culture.** This, as we have seen, can really make a big difference.

- **Root for your country's sports team.** Gilles is very much into soccer, and has been active in recruiting Emma to root for the French team with him. As a consequence, Emma's sports identity is very French for soccer, but Finnish for ice-hockey (the latter is unavoidable when living in Finland).

- **Ensure your children have dual citizenship, if possible.** Having two passports can make a difference in how children identify with their two cultures.

- **Talk about cultural differences.** These could include time management (attitudes towards punctuality), gender roles, family-centeredness, and body language, to name just a few.

Chapter 11.   *Revising the Plan – a personal case study*

So far, we've looked at many ways to encourage bilingualism in our daily lives. You and I both know that as easy as it is on paper, we all have those days and weeks when there just doesn't seem to be time for anything, and it's easy to get sidetracked. I personally checked our own language arrangement last year, and when I noticed that I was not entirely practicing what I preached, I made some changes to our language approach.

You can't add preservatives to language skills; they need to be kept fresh at all times or they will wane. It's the old "use it or lose it" maxim. Writing about the importance of exposing children to their minority language at least 30 percent of the time, I suddenly started wondering about our own case, and what the actual amount of French our children were receiving with the OPOL approach we had been using was. When our children were smaller, we paid a lot of attention to it, but now that they were already very fluent in French, I had the feeling that we had relaxed a bit. I actually *knew* we had, but the question was by how much.

I decided to monitor the situation for a week for the purposes of this book. Since I wasn't the speaker of the minority language, I didn't change what I was doing: I just observed whenever there was interaction in French, and discreetly wrote it down in my notebook.

The first thing I did was to calculate how much French the children had at school. In preschool, nearly all instruction was in French between 8:15a.m. and 1:15 p.m. After this, Sara went to an afternoon club for 4 hours, where everybody spoke Finnish, which pretty much evened out the French/Finnish ratio by the time she was picked up by her dad. Emma's fourth-grade timetable showed that she had 14.5 hours in French each week versus 12.5 hours in Finnish. One of the classes was taught in both languages, but during the breaks between classes, the students tended to use Finnish. Add the car trips with their dad to and from school, and you might say the girls got about 11-12 (Emma) and 16 (Sara) hours of French per week from their school activities.

From the first day of monitoring this, I had to decide what exposing the children to French at least 30% of their waking hours actually meant. Did it mean just being at home hearing other people speak the language? Or playing with your toys while Dad listens to the radio in French? This might count for some exposure, but of course, the impact is a lot stronger if as much of this 30 percent as possible comes from actual interaction between people.

I noticed that unless we actually planned for French to be used with the children, there was very little of it. Coming home from school, the girls had soccer practice, music lessons, or they just disappeared into their rooms to do homework or play – most of which was in Finnish. Gilles and I would cook, we would eat (obviously, there was some interaction there, but not all in French). On many evenings, the kids would still play until we noticed it was time to go to bed, and then there was only time for a quick story. We hadn't given stories up, but they had become shorter and shorter over time.

Actual time spent interacting in French was around one hour most evenings, rarely more. Granted, our situation was saved by the French provided by the school and by activities in French during the weekend, and we reached the 25 hours. Still, the amount of Finnish was more than double that of French.

The following week, I let my husband in on my experiment and asked him that we both make a conscious effort to increase French interaction in our home. The first evening, I cooked while Dad played a great storytelling game called *Il était une fois* with the children. On Tuesday evening, I attended a workshop and Dad asked the kids to help him with the cooking. The next two nights, we took turns with the kids, doing separate activities so that they would both have several hours of alone time with Dad in French. We also reminded their French grandparents to call Emma on Skype in the afternoon, which they did. In the evenings, we planned time for a longer story in French. On Friday evening, we watched a French movie together, and there was a lot of discussion and interaction about it afterwards, in which I too participated in French. Speaking French with my family at the dinner table, I suddenly noticed that what had seemed artificial and unnatural to me when the children were small was natural and easy now that they were older. I even thought about us becoming a full-on mL@H family, but changed my mind after an encounter with our moody preteen. The mom-daughter situation was difficult enough in Finnish without her correcting my gender use in French in the middle of an educational talk on manners. So I might not switch completely, but I don't see any reason not to speak French when the whole family is together.

On Saturday evening, we invited some French friends for dinner. We had been meaning to invite them for a while, but had never seemed to find the time until now, as we were looking for more interaction with French-language contacts. On Sunday, we skyped with the children's French grandparents and planned the coming summer vacation. Doing the math on Sunday evening again, the situation seemed very different compared to the week before. We didn't count every minute, but we felt pretty confident in our total of at least 30 hours of good interaction in French for both girls that week.

We didn't check the numbers again the week after, as that kind of thing can become quite obsessive and that is not the point. It was just a good reminder to show us that even if we think we're doing everything we need to be doing, the reality might be different. The good news is that with a little bit of planning and paying attention, you can get back on track, and the amount of exposure your children get to the non-community language can be significantly increased.

Chapter 12. *What works for whom, and what part does personality play in it all?*

Many parents find that, contrary to their expectations, children actually come with some inborn characteristics, which can make them very different from their parents and even from their siblings. They often interact very differently with the world around them, and like to do different things than their parents or siblings do.

This also applies to children's bilingual acquisition, and out of the ideas presented in this book, some will work for one child in your family and some for the other one. While there can be many reasons for this, one key element could lie in their different personality types.

Like so often in life, I accidentally stumbled upon a real gem of a book for parents, just when I needed it the most! With two daughters who seemed very different from each other – and one in particular very different from me – I've had many frustrating experiences with ideas that I thought were great, but just didn't cut it with them. I didn't understand why Emma wasn't as enthusiastic as me about all the fun activities I had planned for us. I would talk and she would listen to me, patiently it seemed, give a short answer, and go back to her books. She would, however, love the activity books that I bought for her and spend hours with them. This is why her written French is excellent, whereas Sara, bubbly and eager to communicate, is not as drawn to books, but has always been more fluent in oral expression. Reading *Personality Plus for Parents* by Florence Littauer helped me see that understanding my children's personalities, and what they were motivated by, was an important element in finding activities that they, not just I, liked.

Personality types

In her book, Littauer bases the four main personality types she describes on temperament theories developed already by the ancient Greeks and Romans. I definitely recommend reading the book, but to start with, you can google "personality plus quiz" and check which of the following four personalities is dominant for you and which might be for your child. Here is a brief description and ideas for each personality type – but bear in mind that people are usually a combination of at least two types:

Sanguine – "the fun-loving child". They talk all the time, and are enthusiastic about life and everything in it. Comfortable in social situations, they love adventure and meeting new people. On the other hand, Sanguines don't like routine, have short interest spans and emotional ups and downs. If this sounds like your child, s/he is probably motivated to use the minority language through playgroups, fun and inventive games like storytelling (for example, the game *Once Upon a Time* by Atlas games), theater, planning things to do on a trip to the target country and new, exciting activities (where, if possible, they can be the center of attention).

However, don't be surprised if sanguine children are not interested in activity books or games with many details, or hobbies that require concentrating on the same thing for a long time. Even so, they can still be up for extra school work in the minority language if you make it fun for them, and praise them for their efforts. One of the main motivators for sanguine children is meaningful affection from parents, so make sure you interact with them a lot - and bite your tongue whenever you feel like correcting their grammar or criticizing them. Despite their positive outlook on life, they are easily discouraged if they feel they're not accepted as they are.

Choleric – "the result-loving child". They are determined, impatient, and want to get things done *now* - not tomorrow! Choleric children are natural-born leaders who want to participate in the decision-making process, so let them be part - or better yet, partly in charge - of planning activities. Challenging the choleric child equals creating motivation. Cholerics are competitive and like power sports and activities in which they can lead others. They like activities where they can be in control and need to make quick decisions. However, they will probably not be motivated to do things they feel they might not be good at – they want to be sure they have a chance to win!

You can motivate your choleric child to use their minority language by making sure activities include goals that are challenging enough, and involve the opportunity to be in charge (within the boundaries of parental leadership, of course). Show a Choleric child that their help is appreciated in whatever it is they're doing: despite over-achievement, there is a constant need for affirmation. Cholerics are able to dream big and work towards long-term results – as long as they can take some instant action towards the goal and achieve small results right away.

Melancholy – "the detail-loving child". A child with this personality type needs to have information and needs it well in advance! They want to know the schedule and be pre-warned if there are people coming over to the house ("Well, it's my house too," said Emma, when I asked her why it was so important for me to tell her if a friend was dropping by to see *me*). Still, the melancholy child probably says "No" at first to everything new that you suggest, but in this case, "no" doesn't really mean "no". It simply means "Let me think about it and get used to the idea". Therefore, you might want to start talking about next summer's camp months before the deadline for registration, and give them an overview of upcoming activities well in advance.

Melancholics like detailed projects, games with clear rules, and excel at things like museum scavenger hunts. They might resist speaking the minority language in public as it draws attention to them. Instead, they like to have time alone with activity books, make lists and just think. Like me, you might be worried that they're a bit anti-social, and try to get them to play more with other children. What I have found is that the Melancholy child really doesn't like talking just for the sake of talking. However, participation is willing (after mulling it over, of course) in activities that involve talking and interacting with others for a purpose. Instead of spending time in a group of people, Melancholy children are more at ease with just one friend at a time, and tend to form deeper friendships.

Phlegmatic – "the peace-loving child". My husband is a peaceful Phlegmatic. His plan for life to be peaceful and quiet went out the door the minute he met me, and left the country when we had our sanguine child Sara – the two of us had a very different agenda! Phlegmatic children are those that everyone likes and who can get along with anyone. They're good listeners and agreeable – nobody picks a fight with a Phlegmatic! The downside of this can be that Phlegmatics often stay outside any involvement: it's easy to ignore them and they don't mind. They can often be unenthusiastic and unmotivated to act; they'd rather stay outside of it all and watch life roll by in front of their eyes like a reality TV show. The good thing is, they'll probably go along with most of the activities you present them with. They just might not participate as much as you'd like, especially if any of it feels like work.

Still, despite these underlying tendencies, there are successful Phlegmatics in all walks of life, who are not just spectators, but active participants in pursuing their dreams and goals. The key here is to find the one thing they're interested in. Unlike Sanguines, who are interested in doing dozens of things at the same time (and might not finish any of them), Phlegmatics are single-interest children. What parents can do here is try to present the child with options, knowing that it might take time until you find the right one that will motivate your child. Be patient and resist the temptation to get them moving by nagging. Instead, encourage your child to evaluate options and make choices, rather than just follow the crowd. Once they find what interests them, they will become active.

Learning types

In addition to finding out your children's personality types, it may be useful to know their learning types as well. A lot more information can be found about this online, but here are a few ideas about different ways of learning and what might help them acquire their languages.

Auditory learners learn best by hearing. They benefit from listening to stories and songs, group activities and reading out loud.

Visual learners need to see what they are learning. Helpful activities connect the language with pictures or written material. They enjoy, for example, drawing, reading, flashcards and DVDs.

Tactile (or kinesthetic) learners respond to movement and touch. They're interested in things they can physically feel and prefer, quite literally, hands-on learning. They're good at sports, acting, and other things that require skilled eye-hand coordination.

As far as I'm aware, the effects of personality types and different learning styles on bilingual acquisition haven't been subjected to a lot of research. However, I have personally found it very useful to get to know my children better this way and understand how we are different, so I can more easily see things from their points of view.

Conclusion

At a lecture I attended on family bilingualism, the host started by saying: "Today we will talk about raising bilingual children and how to deal with this problem." Another mom and I looked at each other and burst out laughing. I may have problems in my life (don't we all!), but raising bilingual children isn't one of them.

Throughout this book, you have probably noticed that I feel very positive about bilingualism. This is because bilingualism has been, and continues to be, an extremely rewarding experience for our family. You may say, and I would have to agree, that circumstances have been very favorable for the development of bilingualism in our family. Our minority language, French, enjoys worldwide prestige, and there are a lot of resources, including free schooling in our case, available in this language. We parents speak both our minority and majority languages fluently, and our two countries are on the same continent. Even so, it has been (and still is) necessary for our family to make bilingualism a priority for our children to be as at ease in both languages as they are today.

It is true that I have concentrated more on the positive, rather than the challenges, in this book. It's not because I've wanted to make everything sound easier than it is. Even in our favorable circumstances, I would never use the word "easy" in this context (or in any other aspect of real-life parenting). Whenever possible, I have tried out the ideas in this book by pretending that I was starting from scratch and our minority language was Danish instead of French. While this little experiment definitely wasn't effortless (for one thing, I don't speak any Danish), it led me to humbly believe that even if your circumstances are not favorable, at least some of the ideas from this book could be incorporated into your family's bilingual journey. I am, however, sorry if you've felt that some of the ideas were out of your reach for any number of reasons. Hearing the stories of parents from diverse countries and cultures who speak many different languages all over the world has helped me look at things from new perspectives, but I have almost surely overlooked the circumstances of some of you. I welcome all feedback at **Annika@be-bilingual.net**. I would also greatly appreciate it if you would be so kind as to leave an honest review of the book on **amazon.com**.

30 fun activities to do in any language

I sincerely thank you for reading my book, and would like to conclude by presenting you with a list of fun activities that involve using a language - any language, anywhere in the world. Let's not underestimate the power of learning through play, and let's make it fun!

1. **Have a furry pet toy** (or a real one!), and pretend that it only speaks the minority language.
2. **Hand puppets** create endless dialogue with your child.
3. **Dress up and act out stories** from books that you read.
4. **Use funny faces and voices** when you read and encourage your child to do the same.
5. **Play bingo and memory games** to introduce new vocabulary. You can easily make these online yourself.
6. **"Find the right object"** (for more than one child). Set two tables with identical objects on each, and go through them so that the children know the names and what the objects are used for. Read a clue for the object and the children race to find the right one, and bring it back first.
7. **Have a word of the day.** You can make this as easy or complicated (with clues) as you'd like.
8. **Hold supermarket scavenger hunts**. Let your children help you find the items on your shopping list.
9. **Attach language themes to weekly activities**: Saturday soccer in Italian or Sunday sewing in English, for instance.
10. **Make puzzles together.** There's a lot of time and opportunity to talk while looking for the right pieces.
11. **Select a letter for the dinner table** and have everyone try to use as many words beginning with that letter as possible.
12. **Invent different definitions for difficult words from the dictionary.** Whoever comes up with the most convincing definition gets a point.

13. **Play "which one is missing?"** Show the child objects (or photos, or cards) and name them together. Ask the child to close his / her eyes, take away one of the objects and have the child guess which one is gone.

14. **Have a "morning song"** or similar that you always sing at a certain moment.

15. **Play "what's the difference?"** Each player asks what the difference between two things is. For example, between a train and a plane, or more inventively, between a Barbapapa and a Smurf.

16. **Tell fill-in stories**. Get your children to help you with the content of stories in the minority language. For example: "Once upon a time there was_____who really liked to_____."

17. **Use word categories**. An adult calls out a word (say, a cat), and the child names the category (animals).

18. **Write poems and rhymes together**. You can make this easier by listing rhyming words beforehand or buying a rhyming dictionary.

19. **Organize a "German weekend" or a vacation camp** with other parents who speak your language. Each day a couple of the parents organize fun activities in that language, for example cooking, singing, playing games, watching videos, etc. Have a big party for everyone at the end.

20. **Make a "mystery box"** with two holes for the hands. Put different objects inside, close the box and let your children try to guess what the objects are using only their hands. You can also ask them to first describe the objects to you using adjectives like soft, hard, round, furry, etc.

21. **Play Broken Telephone** (also called Chinese whispers). This works best when there are several players and the message is whispered from one person to another. The final version is often very different from the original one!

22. **Word guessing game** (like Taboo). The players need to explain the word that is on their card without using that word. To make

it more challenging, increase the number of words they can't use.

23. **Flash card guessing game**. One person has a flash card and the others try to guess what it is by asking questions that can be answered with a "yes", "no", or "more or less." Another, somewhat more difficult, version of this game is the "20 questions."

24. **Strange food restaurant**. Play a game where you have a restaurant and need to come up with the most original menu ever. Encourage the children to invent strange combinations like strawberry and pea soup or garlic and peach ice-cream. Disgusting, but a sure hit with the kids! You can even take this further by acting out a restaurant scene.

25. **Play Simon Says**. There are many international versions of the game, but you can use any name if the game doesn't exist in your language.

26. **The questions game**. No answers allowed, only questions. Try having a dialogue this way!

27. **The adjective game**. Make some popcorn (for instance) and ask the children to try to describe what it's like to someone who's never had it. What does it smell, feel and taste like?

28. **Why do (or don't) you like it?** Here's another one with adjectives. Make a game of explaining why you enjoy something and not something else. "Just because" does not cut it here.

29. **Guess Who**. You can buy the game or make your own (google the instructions for this). Alternatively, make it a "Guess who I am" where one person is impersonating someone else, and the others try to guess who by asking questions.

30. **Get silly with role play**. Play school, have a tea party, be a princess or a fireman – even monsters from outer space will work, provided they use the minority language in their galaxy!

One final quote from Victor Hugo: *All the forces in the world are not so powerful as an idea whose time has come.* Multilingualism is here to stay, and will help our children bridge the gap between people of different origins and cultures. We're on the right track.

Wishing your family an enriching and fun multilingual journey,

Annika Bourgogne

Vantaa, Finland. 9 December 2013.

Annika@be-bilingual.net

Glossary

Balanced bilingual	A person who is as proficient and comfortable using both languages in most situations. Experts agree that this term excludes most bilinguals.
Biliteracy	Being able to read and write in two languages.
Code-switching	Alternating two or more languages when speaking (even within the same sentence).
Community language	The language used by the majority of people outside the home (often the official language of the country). Also called the majority language.
Dominant language	A bilingual person's strongest language. The one that he or she feels most comfortable using in most situations.
Heritage language	See minority language.
Immersion	A situation where only the target language is used. This can, for example, be at an immersion school, camp or when visiting the minority language country.
Majority language	See community language.
Metalinguistic awareness	An understanding of how a language works and what it's made of. A

necessary skill for learning to read and write.

Minority Language

The language which differs from the community language. Also called non-community language It is sometimes called the target language or second language to express the need to reinforce its learning. When called the heritage language, it refers to the person's immigrant background.

Minority language at home

A language approach where the non-community language is used at home by the whole family. Also referred to as mL@H.

Minority language country

A country where the family's minority language is spoken. Also called the target country.

Mixes language policy

A language approach where several languages are used between people without apparent rules. Also referred to as MLP.

Non-community language

See minority language.

One parent-One language

A language approach where each parent speaks a different language with their children. Also referred to as OPOL.

Passive bilingual

A person who understands two languages, but only speaks one. Also called receptive bilingual.

Simultaneous bilingualism	Learning two languages from birth or before the age of three.
Successive bilingualism	Learning the second language later when the first one is already established.
Target language	See minority language.

References

ABDELILAH-BAUER, Barbara (2008) *Le défi des enfants bilingues*. La découverte, Paris.

ABDELILAH-BAUER, Barbara (2012) *Guide à l'usage des parents d'enfants bilingues*. La découverte, Paris.

ANDERSSON, Theodore (1981) *A Guide to Family Reading in Two Languages: the Preschool Years*. University of Texas Press, Austin.

BAKER, Colin (1997) *Key Issues in Bilingualism and Bilingual Education*. 2nd edition. Multilingual Matters Ltd, Clevedon.

BAKER, Colin (2007) A Parents' and Teachers' Guide to Bilingualism. 3rd edition. Multilingual Matters Ltd, Clevedon, Buffalo, Toronto.

BARRON-HAUWAERT, Suzanne (2004) *Language Strategies for Bilingual Families*. Parents' and Teachers' Guides 7. Multilingual Matters Ltd, Clevedon.

BEARDSMORE, Hugo Baetens (1992) *Bilingualism: Basic Principles*. 2nd edition. Multilingual Matters Ltd, Clevedon.

BILINGUAL FAMILY NEWSLETTER, The (2001-2010).Vols 18-27, Nos.3-4. Multilingual Matters Ltd, Clevedon.

COMBLAIN, Annick (1992) *Apprendre une langue étrangère avant neuf ans*. Le français dans le monde. Vol. 250.

CUNNINGHAM-ANDERSSON, Una (1999) *Growing Up with Two Languages*. Routledge, London.

DEPREZ, Christine (1994) *Les enfants bilingues: langues et familles.* Didiers (collection Crédif), Paris.

DESHAYS, Elisabeth (1990) *L'Enfant bilingue.* Robert Laffont, S.A, Paris.

GROSJEAN, Francois (2010) *Bilingual. Life and Reality.* Harvard University Press. Cambridge, Massachusetts, and London, England.

HAGEGE, Claude (1996) *L'Enfant aux deux langues.* Odile Jacob, Paris.

HAMERS, Josiane, BLANC, Michel (1986) *Bilingualité et bilinguisme.* Pierre Mardaga,Bruxelles.

HARDING, Edith, RILEY, Philip (1986) *The Bilingual Family: A Handbook for Parents.* Cambridge University Press, Cambridge.

HOFFMAN, Charlotte (1991) *An Introduction to Bilingualism.* Longman, London & New York.

KABUTO, Bobbie (2010) Becoming Biliterate: Identity, Ideology, and Learning to Read and Write in Two Languages. Routledge, New York.

KING, Kendall, MACKEY, Alison (2007) *The Bilingual Edge: The Ultimate Guide to Why, When, and How.* HarperCollins e-books.

LIETTI, Anna (1994) *Pour une éducation bilingue.* Payot, Paris.

LITTAUER, Florence (2000) *Personality Plus for Parents.* Revell, Grand Rapids.

MERRILL, Jane (1984) *Bringing Up Baby Bilingual.* Facts on File, Inc., New York.

MULTILINGUAL LIVING MAGAZINE, The (2006-2009). Bilingual / Bicultural Family Network, Seattle, WA.

MYERS-SCOTTON, Carol (2006) *Multiple Voices: An Introduction to Bilingualism*. Blackwell Publishing, Oxford.

MYLES, Carey (2003) *Raising Bilingual Children*. Mars Publishing, Inc, Los Angeles.

RAGUENAUD, Virginie (2009) *Bilingual By Choice*. Nicholas Brealey Publishing, Boston, London.

ROMAINE, Suzanne (1989) *Bilingualism*. Basil Blackwell, Oxford.

SAUNDERS, George (1988) *Bilingual Children: From Birth to Teens*. Multilingual Matters Ltd, Clevedon.

SKUTNABB-KANGAS, Tove (1981) *Tvåspråkighet*. Liber Läromedel Lund, Lund.

STEINER, MD Naomi (2008) *7 Steps to Raising a Bilingual Child*. Amacom, New York.

SØNDERGAARD, Bent (1981) *Decline and fall of an individual bilingualism*. Journal of Multilingual and Multicultural Development. Vol 2.

WANG, Xiao-Lei (2008) *Growing Up with Three Languages: Birth to Eleven*. Parents' and Teachers' Guides. Multilingual Matters, Bristol, Buffalo, Toronto.

ZURER PEARSON, Barbara (2008) *Raising a Bilingual Child*. Living Language (A Random House Company), New York.

Made in the USA
Lexington, KY
20 February 2014